MARBLES, MAYHEM AND MY TYPEWRITER

The Unfadable Life of an Ordinary Man

Mano Sabnani

Marshall Cavendish
Editions

Reprinted 2018

Published in 2018 by Marshall Cavendish Editions
An imprint of Marshall Cavendish International

Other Marshall Cavendish Offices:
Marshall Cavendish Corporation. 99 White Plains Road, Tarrytown NY 10591-9001, USA • Marshall Cavendish International (Thailand) Co Ltd. 253 Asoke, 12th Flr, Sukhumvit 21 Road, Klongtoey Nua, Wattana, Bangkok 10110, Thailand • Marshall Cavendish (Malaysia) Sdn Bhd, Times Subang, Lot 46, Subang Hi-Tech Industrial Park, Batu Tiga, 40000 Shah Alam, Selangor Darul Ehsan, Malaysia

Marshall Cavendish is a registered trademark of Times Publishing Limited

National Library Board, Singapore Cataloguing-in-Publication Data

Names: Sabnani, Mano.
Title: Marbles, mayhem and my typewriter : the unfadable life of an ordinary man / Mano Sabnani.
Description: Singapore : Marshall Cavendish Editions, [2018]
Identifiers: OCN 1005636465 | 978-981-4794-28-2 (paperback)
Subjects: LCSH: Sabnani, Mano. | Journalists–Singapore–Biography. | Businesspeople–Singapore–Biography.
Classification: DDC 079.5957–dc23

Cover design by Cheng Puay Koon

Printed in Singapore by Times Printers Pte Ltd

"Mano was a hitchhiker when Singaporean youths compared unfavourably with their Malaysian peers in the adventure sphere. He was a university publication editor when campus life was much more robust than now.

He was an editor and then a CEO-cum-editor in mainstream newspapers at the time of Lee Kuan Yew. He earned a Purple Heart, if such a battlefield decoration had been bestowed then, for a perilously close encounter with Lee, often referred to with irony as the 'honorary editor-in-chief'.

Now out of full-time journalism, he is still in the media, earning attention as an 'activist investor'. In his memoirs, he is once again in activist mode, coming across with many words of avuncular mien. This uncle tells fascinating tales."

— Peter Lim, former Editor-in-Chief of Singapore
Press Holdings' English/Malay newspapers

"Mano Sabnani's memoirs are written simply without pretensions. He describes one of the multicoloured threads which make up the fabric of Singapore society. A Katong boy, he went to Telok Kurau English Primary School, became a student activist at Singapore University, travelled to London on a shoestring without his father's permission, refused a dowry from his wife's family and married in the Wilkinson Road Sikh Temple. A good journalist, he became, first, editor of *Business Times* and, later, of *TODAY*, both of which he made a great success of. That was when I first knew him. Then he moved on to become an activist investor and now has a closed Facebook group called 'Soul of Singapore', reminding us of the importance of health and family, and reflecting on Singapore's future. Mano's book provides an interesting facet of the many which make up the richness of life in Singapore."

— George Yeo, former Foreign Minister of Singapore

CONTENTS

FOREWORD

By Tan Soo Khoon,
Former Speaker of Parliament

I FIRST MET MANO when we were both students at the University of Singapore (now the National University of Singapore). The campus at Bukit Timah was, to put it very simply, a great place for us to gather, spacious enough for students to move around and experience campus life, yet offering a kind of cosiness and intimacy that allowed friendship amongst students to develop and blossom. One such friendship developed over the years between Mano and me, when we were active together in organising activities for the then University of Singapore Students Union (USSU). Although I was Mano's senior by a year, and we were from different faculties, we, as well as many others, still managed to meet almost daily at our favourite haunt, the old Union House Building, a hotbed of student activism. There, over coffee, we would argue about all kinds of big and little matters that seemed to affect us, provoking each other with our verbal jousting. At the end of the day, our idealistic minds would head home, satisfied that we had dissected and solved the problems facing the world.

The friendships that were nurtured in our student days have lasted a lifetime. Today many of us are still in contact with one another. Several regular gatherings every year organised by Mano and a few others are attended by as many as 70 to 80 of us. There is still abundant verbal crossfire on such occasions, at times more heated and charged than when we were young, our minds and thoughts having been further shaped, hopefully for the better, through our life experiences of several decades, and aided possibly by the affordability of alcoholic stimulants. With the help of modern technology we continue to be in close contact on a daily basis on a Whats-App chat group administered by, you guessed it, Mano.

Reading Mano's memoirs does not only evoke memories of days gone by. Apart from revealing some intimate details of his childhood days and his growing pains, Mano gives us much insight into his colourful career as journalist, editor, CEO, financial analyst and commentator on social issues and current affairs. As an active investor, Mano has often taken up the cudgels on behalf of minority shareholders at company AGMs with his incisive questioning and probing of corporate bigwigs, on occasion irking some belligerent ones. Mano's efforts have contributed to a much-needed vigorous and robust scrutiny of corporate affairs.

Mano also recalls his years in the media, sharing with us his thoughts on what he calls "nation-building journalism" and how he feels that with the advent of digital technology and social media, as well as a fast-changing "landscape of the mind", this has to gradually lead to a pushing back of the Out-of-Bounds markers. The position he has staked out is not a novel one. Some will disagree with him, but nevertheless his thoughts on this topical subject will undoubtedly generate further discourse.

FOREWORD

By Professor Victor R. Savage,
Visiting Senior Fellow, S Rajaratnam School of International
Studies, Nanyang Technological University

I HAVE KNOWN MANO for 48 years since we were first-year students in 1969 at the University of Singapore. It is with honour and delight that I write this foreword for his autobiography. As you read this book, you will realise that Mano's emphasis is on friendships, and so this underscores his choice. Our cohort, the famous "Class of 72", continues to meet periodically till today.

I am encouraged when friends decide to write their auto-biographies. For an academic, autobiographies are the first-hand testimonies and experiences which make for primary data in interpreting and analysing issues. We do not have to be political elites or corporate titans to be qualified to write an autobiography. Even ordinary people have interesting stories to tell of their lives. It would be unfortunate to keep personal memories in our eternal box.

Mano, however, is no ordinary person. He was an executive and editor of renowned newspapers in Singapore – the *Business Times* and *TODAY*. His story is interesting because he offers an example of someone who challenged the odds. Someone who studied in a technical school, read Science in university, pursued a career in journalism, specialised in economics and business analysis in the newspapers and successfully amassed his wealth investing in the stock market. Mano demonstrates that he was no perfunctory employee of his companies: he made a difference in the *Business Times* and *TODAY*. When his Hock Lock Siew column on market news appeared in the *Business Times*, investors took it seriously.

Mano's business instincts underscore his Sindhi roots. The Sindhis have entrepreneurship in their DNA and Mano reflected this in his career in the press, DBS and as a consultant for companies. He is also an astute investor in the stock market. Mano still keeps a close watch on corporate affairs in Singapore and whenever he turns up at company AGMs, corporate executives feel uneasy because of his robust questioning of their accounts and balance sheets.

Since university days, Mano has came across as a strong-willed person. Once he has made a decision, it is difficult to change his mind. He is also a determined and focused person. I remember how he canvassed for advertisements for our souvenir programme for Varsity Showtime 1970 from all the offices in High Street. He was stubbornly persistent. Yet as a fellow travel companion with the Class of 72 posse on our many hitchhiking trips to Malaysia, Mano was accommodating, easy to please and adaptable. In our varsity days, we bonded through mischievous pranks, singing bawdy songs, "smelling" the female species, and personal "ragging" beyond the orientation period. Since then, through all that he has achieved, Mano has remained a humble person and a friend you can always count on.

This autobiography is important for three reasons. Firstly, you have a ring-side view of Mano's participation in the government-press relationship at an important stage of Singapore's history. His unvarnished and frank observations add to the Singapore story. Secondly, Singapore's development from Third World to First is enriched by diverse perceptions and interpretations, and Mano offers some pertinent insights, savoury and unsavoury. His unceremonious exit from *TODAY* amidst a cloud of private and public speculations demonstrated Mano was able to rise above the political froth and see the bigger national picture. There might be disappointment but no bitterness. And thirdly, the government's dictating of "nation-building journalism" defined Mano's experiences in the press and a critical stage of the government's controversial relationship with both the local and foreign press.

Many books and papers have been written about Singapore's success story and while the lion's share of the accolades has gone to the founding Prime Minister, Mr Lee Kuan Yew (1923–2015), the Singapore story would be incomplete if other contributors and contributions were left out. These narratives of the Singapore story come from five Ps: personalities, power elites, pressure groups, the press and the public. Mano helps to shed light on the role of the Singapore press in nation building. The press were at the frontline of the political arena and power elites of Singapore, and their experiences carry many of the unwritten narrations of Singapore's national story.

Reading between the lines and within the text, one gets both an overt and nuanced perspective of how government leaders displayed an ambivalent relationship with the press. In the process, Singapore's journalists, working within narrow margins of press freedoms, developed their own brand of journalism. Despite tight restrictions, Mano demonstrates that Singapore reporters managed to excel in reporting and deliver surprising scoops. Pitted against the freedom of the press in India and the Philippines, one can say the Singapore newspapers have done exceptionally well in winning Asian press awards annually in a politically closeted environment.

PREFACE

FOR A WHILE NOW, I have been thinking about writing memoirs and a couple of other books before it is too late. I am already in my 60s, and I'd really like to put my experiences and thoughts down before my memory starts to fade. My intention is simple: to share my life story and my thoughts on various issues and trends, and leave a legacy for my family.

I started work on this book in 2016, following the end of my work with SIM University in April, having served as an adjunct professor and advisor to the Centre for Applied Research and the Business School for about seven years. I had also stepped down from directorships at two companies after some years. Writing fell right into place.

Within these pages are my stories of growing up in Singapore, of finding my footing in the world, and of my experiences as a journalist, editor, investment banker, corporate executive and investor. This book reflects my interests at various stages of my life.

I hope you enjoy reading the book, or at least parts of it. Your thoughts and feedback would be appreciated. I can be reached via email at mano.sabnani@gmail.com. You can also easily connect with me on Facebook (and the related Messenger), where I have an active profile.

My thanks are due to various people who have, in one way or other, inspired or assisted me to put this book together. Margaret Thomas shared her book publication experience generously and made suggestions on the manuscript. Steven Ooi went through the whole book and suggested very useful changes to language and content. Jaime Koh has been a key partner in research and the drafting of the contents. My sincere thanks go to Dr Victor Savage and Tan Soo Khoon for writing forewords for this memoir. Peter Lim and George Yeo kindly consented to write blurbs after reading one of my drafts. Appreciation is also due to Marshall Cavendish for making the publication of this book possible.

Last but not least, my love and appreciation go to my family members – my wife Nisha, my daughter Natasha, and my sons Karan and Dev – who have been supportive all the way and given me their frank opinions and valuable suggestions. This book is dedicated to all of them as well as to the extended Sabnani family and my many friends and relatives who have made my life's journey interesting and enjoyable in a variety of ways. A special dedication is due to my late, unforgettable parents – my father, Pritamdas K Sabnani, and my mother, Janki P Sabnani.

THE POWER WITHIN

ON THE MORNING of 17 April 2015, I had a few questions on my mind as I headed to Singapore-listed Noble Group's Annual General Meeting (AGM) as a shareholder. The company had recently come under attack for its accounting policies and disclosure.

Starting in February that year, a small research company – Iceberg Research – had issued a series of reports on the commodity trading firm, stating that it substantially over-valued its assets, under-reported its debts, and overvalued its contracts. This started a chain of events which saw the public questioning the company's ethics, its accounting practices and even the competence of its management. In early April, US short-seller Muddy Waters Research issued a report casting doubt over Noble's cash flow and management. Noble's credentials and share price took a hit.

At the AGM, Noble's founding chairman Richard Elman ruled that he would not answer any questions relating to the Iceberg or Muddy Waters reports. "We consider the Iceberg matter finished. We have started legal proceedings and we look forward to challenging their inaccurate, unreliable and misleading claims in a public court. We don't think there is a better venue to challenge these allegations than in front of a judge in a court which is open to the public," he said. He added that "the recent Muddy Waters report barely dignifies a response. It was short, it re-hashed an old allegation, it contained no new evidence and it used a very absurd behavioural analysis of one analyst phone call... We will not be revisiting details of these allegations in this meeting."

To my mind, Elman's response was too sweeping as the matters raised in the reports were linked to the company's accounts, and so they should be rightly raised to the board on how the issues reflected or affected the developments in the group.

Earlier in the meeting, I had asked questions about the accounts and profits of the company. Later, one shareholder raised a question about the group's stake in the Australian coal company Yancoal, and how its value had crashed due to the slump in the price of coal. Elman put him down and refused to answer the question: "Does it have to do with the financial statement? If it does, I'll answer it. But if it doesn't, we won't, OK. We have to stick by the rules and regulations that the meeting is being run by. Please."

I intervened and supported the shareholder, Joseph Lau, as the question was relevant, given that Noble had a stake in Yancoal. I told Elman: "I think you are too defensive today... you are unnecessarily defensive, and in denial mode. I mean, why don't you open up? Relax, you know. If you are not guilty of anything, why are you so uptight?"

Elman did not take too kindly to my intervention and the applause it got from the other shareholders.

Elman: "I would like to repeat. We are talking about the audited financial statement and reports of the directors and auditors. If it's relative to that, we will absolutely answer the question."

Mano: "I mean, you have not even let him ask the question. I'm just getting this feeling that you've all come here just to get it over with."

Elman: "I remember you from last year. The first criticism you had was the font on the screens was too small, you couldn't see them. You remember that?"

Mano: "Yes!"

Elman: "Are they big enough now?"

Mano: "Your annual report is very badly done – look at the typeface, look at the..."

Elman: "It's very badly done. Thank you. Moving on. So let's have the Yancoal question. Alright. Let's have the Yancoal question, OK."

*   *   *

Over the years, I have been involved in many such exchanges with company chairmen who were not friendly or not open with shareholders about relevant issues. I have not been afraid to raise hard questions, be it at AGMs, through letters to the press or directly with the relevant institutions.

In 2012, I was instrumental in the Singapore Stock Exchange (SGX) moving in on the Blumont, LionGold and Asiasons blowup. Blumont was a Singapore-based investment company, and it was considered a penny stock. In June 2011, it was priced at about 2 cents a share. But by June 2013, it was trading at $2.45. That rise defied logic as there was almost zero fundamental basis for it, and I sensed that all was not well. I wrote to SGX to alert them to this anomaly.

In October that year, Blumont's shares, together with two other penny stocks, LionGold and Asiasons, crashed, wiping more than S$5 billion off their market value. SGX suspended the trading of these stocks soon after. These stocks were linked by cross-shareholdings and office holders. The bubble was probably created by manipulation of trades. The suspected mastermind behind this blowup in stock prices and subsequent collapse, Malaysian businessman and speculator Soh Chee Wen, is, at the time of writing, facing charges for the whole episode which set the Singapore stock market back a few years.

In April 2016, I wrote a letter to the Singapore *Business Times* about the Osim International buyout errors. Earlier in March, Osim's founder and major shareholder Ron Sim sought to acquire the shares that he did not already own to take the company private. Sim's advisor, Credit Suisse, made a mistake in buying shares above the takeover price. That same morning, the parties admitted the mistake and had to increase the takeover price by two cents, as they had bought two cents higher than the offer price. How it happened was that the stock had gone ex-dividend of two cents the previous day and they had been accumulating shares in the market at the takeover price. Credit Suisse apparently did not realise the ex-dividend status and continued to buy at the offer price, when they should only have bought two cents lower than the previous day's price. As a result, it cost Ron Sim two cents more per share to take over the minorities. It added up to millions of dollars.

It is, perhaps, for these instances that the media has labelled me an "activist investor".

I did not set out to be an activist. My training and experience as a business journalist and Head of Research at DBS have a big part to play. When being presented with a situation, I tend to have questions. Before going to any AGMs, I read through the companies' annual reports and jot down any questions I have, so that I can go prepared. Asking questions is a natural and instinctive part of how I operate. It is not my intention to provoke, but to seek clarifications. I do not go to AGMs for free food and drinks. I do not write letters or speak to the press to be in the spotlight. In recent years, many fellow shareholders have been messaging me to ask questions at the AGMs on their behalf. They feel that they do not have the standing to ask questions, especially when faced with strong personalities like Noble chairman Elman.

As an investor, I take an active interest in the health and development of the companies I invest in. The questions I have cover a broad spectrum of a listed group's business and management. What are the key issues at stake: Is it debts? Is it governance? Is the core business shrinking? If so, what is being done? I have no intention of embarrassing anyone. In any event, I take a polite approach and avoid making defamatory statements. Every question I ask or statement I make is based on the materials presented and the situation at hand. The questions clarify any doubts shareholders have, and only serve to help us understand the business and company better. Sometimes, I don't just ask questions but I also offer suggestions. Some companies do appreciate it, and they don't go into attack mode.

Investing has been – and still is – a big part of my life. I bought my very first stock in the 1970s, when I was doing my National Service. That was a disaster but it spurred me to learn more about stocks, shares and the market. That knowledge was cemented through my subsequent years in *Business Times*, DBS, and the corporate world. Today, I spend a large part of my day on investing and corporate advisory work through my own company, Rafflesia Holdings Pte Ltd.

Even though I have retired from newspaper publishing, writing continues to be a big part of my life. Through Rafflesia, I've completed a book for Keppel Corporation. I've also completed a book on the concept and development of Singapore's sixth university, SIM University (now Singapore University of Social Sciences), on the occasion of its 10th anniversary. My daily routine includes writing on Facebook, where I started and manage two pages: "Soul of Singapore" and "Manologue". Soul of Singapore is a closed group of about 8,000 members who discuss various issues, notably those concerning my small city-state. The members are mostly my friends and contacts. Manologue is a fun blog on life matters and some humour as well as puzzles, with more than half a million followers.

Several years ago, as an adjunct professor at SIM University and advisor to the university's Centre for Applied Research, I had the opportunity to do a study on local companies to suss out their success factors. The work covered more than 30 companies listed on the Singapore Exchange. I personally interviewed the leaders of these companies. It led me to the conclusion that people count in the end. In successful organisations, the right leaders with correct values and ability will ensure problems are resolved as quickly as possible and operations carry on smoothly. Good people at the top also ensure that their values and priorities are passed down to rank and file, so that the whole organisation moves in tandem.

It is the same with individuals. How can you achieve what you set out to do with your life? What is required to get somewhere and for you to be able to look back on your life with satisfaction at different stages? There are many life coaches out there, and many gurus and advisors offering all sorts of pointers on all aspects of life. For me, the essence is integrity and ability.

Anyone can live a life of integrity. It is a question of whether you want to do it. Valuing integrity highly means you work and live in a way that you do not trample on others along the way. You do an honest job each day of your life and you avoid short-changing anyone. Pay people their dues and if you have borrowed from individuals or institutions along the way, you repay them in full.

Living a life of integrity means you can look back at any time and say all your savings and assets were earned in an honest way and were well-deserved. You will gain much internal satisfaction and peace if you can say that to anyone with hand on heart. You will be able to sleep well with a clear conscience.

To succeed in what you set out to do with your life at any stage, you have to have some ability. Here, the secret lies in knowing what are your strengths. Know what you enjoy doing or have a passion for and see if that can be turned into a business or profession. It does not really matter if others have the same passion or ability and may compete with you.

This is The Power Within that you need to bring out. The important thing is to know yourself and to be honest in self-assessment. Keep learning and improving yourself and realising innate abilities which may not be so obvious at first. There are people who develop late in life, meaning they discover new talents as they go along. So do not give up on yourself but know yourself and your strengths each step of the way.

Life can be enjoyable and fruitful. But it is not a bed of roses for most of us. As you will see in the story of my life, the road to where I am today was by no means straightforward or easy. We have to work to get somewhere. To get somewhere, we have to solve problems along the way. In order to overcome obstacles, we have to have thinking abilities. These problem-solving abilities can also be developed. They are valuable skills that are useful throughout our lives.

Chapter 1

A BOY IN JOO CHIAT

I WAS TOLD my birth brought good luck to the family.

By the time I was born in 1950, my family had moved into a two-bedroom rented apartment in the middle-class area of Joo Chiat. It was an upgrade from the rented room my parents and my two older brothers had lived in. The new place, Gian Singh Flats, had two bedrooms, a living room, a dining room and a balcony. The toilets were shared, but it was a generous space for a young family.

At that time, my father, Pritamdas K Sabnani, was working in the textile industry, and he was doing well. He had come to Singapore from Bombay in 1941 to fulfil his three-year contract as a salesman in a Sindhi textile firm in High Street. Originally from the Sindh province in present-day Pakistan, my father had moved to Bombay in search of better prospects. All his brothers had similarly left home for Bombay by then. Sindh was part of the British Empire, first under the British East India Company, then as a separate province under British India. By the 1930s, life in Sindh was becoming difficult, with increasing lawlessness. Some quarters then were fighting for independence from the British, and some of the Muslim population were fighting for greater Muslim autonomy. Dada used to tell stories of young Hindu girls in Sindh Province being kidnapped and forcibly converted to Islam. For him, Bombay was an opportunity to make something of himself.

In Bombay, my father worked for a textile shop, and he also got married. When he came to Singapore, he had to leave behind his new bride, 18-year-old Ishwari Khemlani. (Her name was changed after marriage, in accordance with Hindu Sindhi tradition, to Janki P Sabnani.) They were matchmade, and had married just the year before. He was due to return to Bombay after his Singapore contract was up. But the Japanese Occupation (1942–45) threw a spanner in the works; he was left stranded in Singapore.

During the war, my father – we called him Dada – worked as a textile supplier to the Japanese. It was circumstantial. There was business opportunity, and in those terrible times, the Japanese preferred to deal with the non-Chinese. Dada was in the right place at the right time, an opportunity in crisis. He used to tell us he made good money and that he was able to purchase a few properties. But he lost it all when the war ended. The Japanese "banana notes" that were in circulation then were rendered worthless, and the properties sold during the Occupation reverted to their original owners. Dada had a whole drawer of banana notes, with which my brothers and I used to play Monopoly. Once, I asked Dada why he was keeping the notes, and he said, "One day they will reimburse me." That day never came.

So Dada started from scratch again after the war. One of the first things he did when the Japanese Occupation ended was to return to Bombay to reunite with my mother. He brought her over to Singapore and it was here that they started a new life. Dada worked full-time as a textile merchant while my mother devoted herself to the home. My older brothers Chandru and Shanku were born in 1947 and 1948. I arrived in 1950. Two younger siblings followed, my brother Ramesh in 1952, and my sister Nimu in 1955. A baby was stillborn in 1959.

My mother had her hands full taking care of a young and growing brood. She spent mornings and afternoons doing the chores around the house, with the help of a maid, and solving any problems arising with us children. But she also led a balanced life, maintaining a healthy social circle. After a short nap in the afternoon, she would be off in the evening, around 5 p.m., to go for a walk with her friends or to enjoy a chat-and-tea session. She would be usually home by 6.30 p.m., in time to check that all was well with the children and to prepare dinner for the family. Dada would usually return home at 8 p.m. and join us for dinner. After dinner, we would all would sit in the sitting room or lounge area and chit-chat or read, or entertain any guests we had.

This traditional division of roles served us well. Our family life was fairly stable, and my father did not see the need for Mum to earn another income. Having Mum at home was great for maintaining family well-being. Her soft

My parents, Pritamdas K Sabnani and Janki P Sabnani, in Katong Park, 1958.

Cousin Kishin Balani carrying my sister Nimu; the boys in front are (left to right) my brothers Chandru, Ramesh, Shanku, and myself.

approach with the children worked well in creating harmony in the family as it grew to embrace seven very different persons, including four often-raucous boys and a young sister. Mum was kind and gentle, and she would tip us off if Dada was upset about something, so that we would do the right thing and not agitate him further.

Dada worked hard at providing for the growing family. He started a small business doing textile indenting. Essentially he was a commissioned agent for suppliers. He would help source for buyers, to whom the suppliers would then sell the goods. Later, he started a shop at Anson Road called Stylo. The shop, located where IBM Building is today, was a small departmental store of sorts, catering mostly to the merchant sailors in the area. He sold everything from cameras to kimonos, to souvenirs of all sorts. The hours were long and the work was hard. Dada gave up the shop in 1970, and went to work at the New India Emporium at High Street, retiring in 1990 at the age of 70.

Tragically, my mother passed away in 1963 as a result of complicated childbirth. She was only 40 years old. She had had a stillborn baby in 1959 and by the time she conceived again in 1963, the child had to be delivered by caesarean. It was to be her second one as the stillborn baby was also a caesarean baby. In those days, having a second caesarean was considered risky. She was not in good health – during her pregnancy, she had high blood pressure and diabetes, and she could hardly walk. But she insisted on going through with the birth because she said every child was a gift from God, and she would carry it to full term. When she went into labour, the doctor told us, very frankly, that it would be between her and the child.

Mum passed away the day after giving birth to my youngest brother, Vijay.

Vijay was considered a blue baby, and had to be put in intensive care in hospital. He only came home a week later. By then, as according to Hindu customs, Mum's funeral was over and she had been cremated. So within a short time, we had to make major adjustments to our lives, grieving for our mother who had been a large part of our lives and taking care of a new baby. Mum's passing was traumatic for all of us, as we had grown to depend on her for a stable family life. She was the one who used to initiate going for community events or to the temple. With her gone, our family became less plugged in with the greater Sindhi community, especially with Dada having to earn a living and manage a family.

Dada became more involved with us. He would often make breakfast for us before leaving for work. When there were issues to be dealt with – like sick children, or school matters – he would be on hand to sort things out. It affected his work.

The older children all had to chip in to help with the newest addition to the family. We had a good Chinese servant who helped with the housework. When Dada went to work, we older boys, then teenagers, took turns taking care of the younger children – our eight-year-old sister and the newborn baby – depending on our schooling schedule. That made us all a little more mature. Our youngest brother grew up to be very independent and very successful.

For many years, we made the arrangement work. When Mum died, Dada said he did not want to marry again, even though Mum's sister said he should, if he could. But he said no. For about 10 years, Dada played the dual role of father and mother to us five. One day in 1973 – I was in university at that time – Dada introduced me to his friend, Sita. He said he wanted to marry her, and he asked for my thoughts (he had already spoken to my elder brothers). I said if she would make him happy, why not? After all, he had been on his own for almost 10 years then. That year, Dada and Sita married.

I have a lot of respect for my stepmother. She is half-Chinese but she followed my father's Indian ways, in terms of customs, religion and habits. She was a good stepmother to us and a good wife to my father. They have two sons, Anil and Haresh, who are now bosses of the very successful Spize Restaurants in River Valley, Bedok Marketplace and the Temasek Club in Rifle Range Road.

Dada passed away in 2008, at the age of 88. He was a hard worker who sought to run his life in a caring, honest way. The way he lived his life had an impact on me. He was always there for us in whatever situation. He was prudent with expenses, but not stingy, he was God-fearing, and he was careful with diet and exercise. I have sought to live my life according to his motto: "Simple living and high think-ing". What this means is to live simply, based on needs rather than wants. Avoid unnecessary expenditure and save for the future. At the same time, we should be available to friends and family members in need of help. High thinking means seeing the big picture of life and not getting carried away by daily events. Have your own rational principles and values and live by them, as far as possible. We all make mistakes – that is fine, so long as you try your best and avoid making the same mistakes again.

Perhaps the strongest legacy Dada left was his belief that "You've got to look after your family". Unity among siblings is very important. It is what gives the family strength. I want my children to remember that, and I try to show them by exam-ple, not just through words. There haven't been any serious disputes among my siblings since my parents passed away. The reality is that in spite of parents' best intentions, some families break apart and siblings experience bitter feuds. It is sad that Singapore's first family has fractured appallingly following the passing of the much-respected head. I think parents have to try harder to prevent this.

My belief in looking after one's family is why I continue to provide financial support for my younger brother Ramesh (fourth among five boys), who has always been a little slow in carrying out daily activities. He is a smart person and can be very logical, but there are some social situations that he just cannot handle. As a young boy, he had a hot temper and had occasional fights with Dada and the neighbours. Dada took him to see various doctors, who said he could be suffering from manic depression and slight schizophrenia. Nisha, my wife, is also very good with him, visiting him regularly to make sure he is taking care of himself and eating properly.

Boyhood

I spent the bulk of my childhood in the Joo Chiat/Telok Kurau area. In the 1950s and 1960s when I was growing up, it became a tinderbox when some of the socio-political unrest between the Chinese and Malay communities spilled into the area. There was the inevitable fighting, from time to time, between the two groups during those turbulent years. There were also some localised curfews. But by and large, Joo Chiat was a peaceful neighbourhood where I spent some of the best times of my early life.

Like my elder brothers, I attended Telok Kurau English Primary School at Lorong J Telok Kurau from 1957 to 1962. It was a feeder school to Raffles Institution and the school where our founding Prime Minister, Lee Kuan Yew, had his primary education. But the chief reason my father chose to send us boys to the school was that it was close to home, and that reduced the cost of transport. Conveniently, I inherited my brothers' uniforms. Later, the school was renamed Telok Kurau East School when the new Telok Kurau West School was opened. The West School, akin to today's Northlight

School, was built to take in overaged students who were in the slower stream as well as repeat students.

I was quite excited on my first day of school. I remember Dada walked me to the bus-stand near our house where I got on the bus (Singapore Traction Company bus number 22) that would take me to my school. In my time, the school was just a two-storey wooden structure. The classroom blocks and the office surrounded the school field in a broad U-shaped formation. I remember going to class on the first day and making a few friends. My earliest friends were a pair of Malay twins, Mahmud and Salleh, two Chinese boys by the names of Lim and William Ang, and South Indians Patkunan and Gunaseelan.

In those days, the school's principals were typically Ceylonese-Tamils. Ratna Sabapathy was the principal during my time. He was known as a strict and stern man, as were some of the teachers. Once, I was lured into playing soccer with a few boys. It was the school holidays and we decided to play in the school field. The gate was open, and nobody would mind, so we thought. Within minutes, the Senior Master (discipline master) came and rounded us up and told us off for using the field without permission. We were given a caning and sent home. We felt the caning was unjustified: we had not done anything wrong nor did we damage anything. We did not know the staff were in that day, working. The principal was in that day too. We went home with sore bottoms, and kept it from our parents.

Telok Kurau English School had always been a boys' school offering the usual range of subjects, including English, Mathematics, Science, History, Geography and Second Language. Tamil was an option but my siblings and I chose Malay, which uses the romanised script and which we felt was more adaptable for us. The Sindhi language was not offered; in any case the script is very different from Tamil. My favourite subjects in primary school were English and History, which I did well in.

Kites, marbles and hantam bola

I was not the most sporty among my friends, but like most boys of my generation, I liked a good game of *hantam bola*, marbles and kite-flying. *Hantam bola* involved a group of children, usually boys, using a ball to hit each other. Anyone who got hit by the ball had to then hold on to it until he could hit another boy with it. It was a fast and tiring game that could be played in any open group. Marbles involved glass or stone marbles played on sandy ground. The objective was to try and hit and push as many other marbles into a sandy hole dug by the players. The winning marble would be the one left outside the hole.

Kite-flying was my one-time obsession. I was about 9 or 10 years old when I got into kites, and soon I was flying them at every opportunity I could get – after school and most days during the school holidays. I wanted to get better at flying, and I wanted nicer kites. I started small, playing with bought kites. Then I started making my own, with my own designs and engineering, if you can call it that, with bits of tracing paper, and bamboo or cane strips. I went as far as making my own glass-coated thread that was so popular then for kite-fighting. Together with my brothers and friends, we would source for unwanted glass lightbulbs or fluorescent light tubes, crush them and mix the shards with starch to coat the strings which we attached to the kites. I learned the art of coating the thread from my downstairs neighbours, Ah Chew and Ah Kow.

Kite-fighting was the "in" thing. Armed with our kites and glassed-up threads, we'd go hunting for other kites. We usually never knew which kite belonged to whom. Cutting down a kite and watching it fly away was all part of the fun. When we spotted a kite we wanted to cut, we would take aim and try to bring it down. Of course, I didn't like my kites being cut, but that was part and parcel of the game. When that happened, I had to start all over again.

Sometimes fights and arguments would arise. "Ooi! Don't cut my kite lah," some of the boys would shout if they realised their kites were targets. But most of the time, the cutters would not care. They'd continue to aim for the targeted kite, and when the kite was cut, all the kids would shout "Liao! Liao! Liao!" (Hokkien for "finished") and rush for the fallen kite like it was gold. Any kite flying in the sky was free game. We'd see where it was flying and calculate the rough trajectory it would take. When we were out of money to buy kites or materials to make kites, we'd go out and wait for falling kites. It was finders keepers. We boys would sometimes fight over the kite – "Oooi! Mine! Mine!" Whoever picked up the fallen kite was the owner. It was exhilarating to win at kite-flying.

I was in Primary Five then, and I was flying every spare moment I had, to the point that it affected my results. My Mum warned me about getting carried away with the habit. That was when I decided to scale back on it.

In our spare time, my brothers and friends and I would also go fruit hunting. That was really another term for stealing fruits. In our neighbourhood, many families grew fruit trees in their gardens. We would go along the back lanes and pick the low-hanging fruits – starfruit, rambutans, mangoes. Some neighbours didn't mind us picking the fruits that were outside their compounds. Once, my eldest brother went so far as to go into someone's garden when he spotted some ripe fruits. Unfortunately, the dog spotted him before he could get to his target, and he was chased out, but not without incurring a bite on his leg.

Cycling was another favourite activity. We used to rent second-hand bikes from the neighbourhood "Ah Pek's" (old man's) bike shop and then cycle around the Joo Chiat-Haig Road area. My parents always reminded us to stay off the roads. In those days before the Haig Road flats were built, there were a lot of open spaces where we could cycle.

Those were relatively carefree days, and our friendships were good. We would invite one another over for festivities – Chinese New Year, Hari Raya, and Deepavali.

School was never as high-pressured as it is today. I was diligent about my work but kept largely to myself. I was more introverted when I was young, and did not project myself too much. I remember one of my teachers commented in my report book, "Too quiet in class". I wasn't confident in speaking up in public, I was nervous. Then, subsequently, another teacher wrote, "Naughty at times". You just can't win.

Di Tanjong Katong

I took my PSLE in 1962, and with my results I could qualify for Raffles Institution. But Dada was concerned about the extra cost of travel, and since my older brothers were in Tanjong Katong Secondary Technical School, that was where I went too. It was nearby and it was a good school. I had no regrets as I had a great time at Tanjong Katong. It broadened my horizons and set the foundation for many things to come.

One of my best experiences in secondary school was joining the Boy Scouts. Some of my good friends were in the Scouts and they got me to join them. Being in Scouts taught me the value of being prepared. I'd rather be prepared for whatever situation than wait for it to happen and then try to solve it. It has since become very much part of my psyche and a principle I continue to follow to this day.

Primary Six class at Telok Kurau English School, 1962, with our form teacher, Mr D'Costa; I'm standing sixth from the right.

With fellow Boy Scouts of 93rd Seladang Scouts Troop, on a raft we built, in the sea off Telok Paku (Changi), 1964. I'm the third from the right (looking pensive!). Tay Boon Hong and M Narayanan are seen "rowing" the raft with bamboo poles while Sundarajoo waves and Raymond Lim falls backwards into the water.

Being in the Scouts also taught me a good measure of independence. My parents were initially worried about the potential dangers and risks that I would be exposed to. They always told me not to take unnecessary risks. Take water for instance. My father always said being near a pool of water was dangerous for me. But I told him that by learning how to swim I would become resilient, and water would not be that dangerous any more. It took a bit of persuasion but my parents eventually relented.

Joining the Scouts also polished up my outdoor skills and helped me grow some confidence. As Scouts, we took many tests, and learned teamwork, helping one another. I enjoyed the activities – the camping, cycling trips, and swimming excursions, for instance. Until then, I was a relatively protected middle-class boy who spent more time indoors than out. Being in the Boy Scouts drew me out much more and I made some good friends along the way.

Besides studying and Scouting, I began to become more involved with activities such as writing for the school magazine and debating. I was not on the school magazine committee but I remember contributing articles such as one on Beatlemania, which was sweeping the world, Singapore included, at that time. It was one of my earliest tastes of "journalism", if you like. I also once tried my hand at Talentime, but alas, I didn't quite make it.

My Secondary Four form teacher, Mr Thomas Tan, encouraged us to speak in front of the class. He was trying to encourage us to develop critical thinking and debating skills, as well as brush up on our public speaking. This provided the foundation for later on when I stood for student council and student union elections at university. Speaking in public was really more a confidence-building exercise for me. I'd read up on how to be confident in public speaking. One of the things I found out is that you have to be confident in yourself first. If you keep thinking that your audience is smarter than you or knows more than you, you won't feel confident. You have to tell yourself that people in your audience may be smart, but you have a point to make. If you have a point and you make it well, it will be well received whether you are right or wrong. There's no right or wrong, sometimes.

The arts and humanities were always my strongest suit – English, Literature, History. I always scored well for these subjects. But instead of pursuing them, I ended up in the Science and Technical streams in Tanjong Katong. For the Cambridge O-level exams, I did Technical Drawing, Metal Work, Physics, English Literature, History and Maths. I had to put in extra effort for the non-humanities subjects, while History was entirely self-taught as the school did not offer any lessons. I scored A1 for History and an overall Division One in the exams.

Hitchhiking in Malaysia

After my O-levels in 1966, I did a three-week hitchhiking trip to Malaysia with a friend, David Low Keng Soo. That was my very first overseas trip. David and I were close friends, and we had heard people talking about hitchhiking in Peninsular Malaysia. I had not seen the world, never stepped outside of Singapore. Hitchhiking was an attractive option for us. We were young and did not have a lot of money. Travel was a luxury in those days that not many could afford. We decided to give it a go.

David and I started our trip at Rochor, where we took a bus up to Bukit Timah and started hitchhiking from there. In those days, some of the Malaysian drivers were more amenable to picking up hitchhikers. One of the things about hitchhiking is that you have to be patient. Sometimes 30 to 40 cars will pass you by, even on quiet roads, before you get a ride. On occasion, if we were lucky, we could hitch a ride direct to our destination. At other times we'd just be dropped wherever it was convenient for the driver, and then wait for another pickup.

Our trip took us to Muar, Batu Pahat, Malacca, Kuala Lumpur (KL), Cameron Highlands, Ipoh, Penang and Pulau Langkawi.

One of the memorable events was being picked up in a big, posh car. I think it might have been Ghafar Baba, the Malaysian politician. We were chatting in the car and he was asking about our trip. Then his tone changed when we said we were from Singapore. He was not that fond of Singapore, and he turned cold.

Most of the Malaysians we met on the trip were down-to-earth and friendly. We were picked up by a guy driving a Volvo enroute to KL. He was fast and efficient, and we stopped for a break at a famous duck noodle shop, and he bought us food, seeing that we did not have much to spend. Most of the time, on our trip, people would buy us food. Some drivers would also give us tips. One of the things we learned was to look to police stations or fire stations, especially outside the city area, for accommodation. Usually they'd have bachelor quarters and if there was room, they'd put us up there. We spent a number of nights in such accommodation in various Malaysian towns. That not only saved us a lot of money, it also allowed us to experience how ordinary Malaysians lived.

When we were in Perlis, the fire brigade bunk was full, so we took shelter at a mosque. The janitor allowed us to sleep on the verandah, which was sheltered. In the middle of the night, we were woken up by some guy, probably the imam. He asked where we were from and whether we were Muslims. I told him we were from Singapore, non-Muslims, and he said we could not sleep at the mosque. He drove us out. At times like these, we were forced to spend some money on hotels.

Our favourite parts of the trip were the times we spent in the small towns and villages. The children would come out and see what these two foreigners were doing in their place, and we'd just chat. Many of the villagers would also extend a helping hand when we needed it. In Penang, we went up Penang Hill on the funicular railway and then decided to trek down through the jungle. We totally underestimated the trek and were not well equipped with water and food. Along the way, we had to ask families living there for water. Some gave us biscuits and other small snacks to eat. We were very touched by their friendliness and generosity. In Cameron Highlands, I remember, we were deciding what to have for lunch at the tuckshop at the bus station. It was the cheapest place to eat. We didn't have much and were deciding if we should share a plate of chicken rice. A stranger overheard us and ordered food for us, one set each. We accepted with much gratitude.

At Kek Lok Si Buddhist Temple – one of the largest in Malaysia and set in Air Itam in Penang, overlooking the sea – we stumbled upon a man sitting in one of the pavilions on the floor and shuffling playing cards around. One simply had to guess which of the three cards was the Jack of Spades. The minimum bet was $5. People were playing and winning. We joined in too, thinking it could earn us extra pocket money. David played and won initially. It seemed so easy. But soon after, he lost and so did I. By then, I was down to my last $15 for the trip as I had lost $5. He had a little more, after losing $20. It was only much later that we realised it was all a trick. People were betting – were they stooges? – and we naively joined. The experience was painful because $5 was a good quarter of my remaining travel budget. After that we were really broke. I was down to my last dollars by the time we reached the then exotic island of Langkawi, the last stop of our trip.

At that time, Langkawi was really remote, and the town of Kuah was essentially only a street with two rows of shops. The cheapest place to eat was the Indian bakery. We got a huge loaf of bread for 20 cents. We sat on the beach and relaxed. David managed to climb a short coconut tree and we used our daggers to prise open the coconut and devour its contents. We were Boy Scouts with an adventurous spirit, trying to make the best of the time and to enjoy it. We were in Langkawi during the Muslim fasting month and were lucky to be invited by the local firemen to join them for the evening break-fast dinner. That was such a feast for us.

When it was time to go home we didn't want to spend money on the boat. We didn't have much left. We found a Shell Company fuel tank ferry that was heading back to the mainland. We spoke to the ferry hand who agreed to take us. When it was time, we were at the pier and we hopped onto the boat. We had the shock of our lives: there was a coffin on board! They were bringing the coffin back to the mainland. We didn't have a choice, so we sat next to the coffin for the next three hours or so, with cockroaches running at our feet. That was another shock – we had not expected the speed (or the lack of it) of the journey. When we reached Kuala Perlis, it was at an unearthly time. We hitched a ride with the boat crew on their truck towards Kuala Lumpur, where we took a break before hitchhiking back to Singapore via Malacca.

That was an unforgettable trip. Later, in university, I was able to use my skills and experience when a group of us hitchhiked to Cameron Highlands. I taught my friends the tips and tricks of hitchhiking, including where to wait, what to look out for and what not to do. You have to pick your spot to wait. Generally, clear roads are the best. It's best not to wait at major roads with turnings and flyovers, because you won't actually know where the vehicles are going. Waiting by a road with a clear direction is the best. That's when the motorists can spot you and there are not so many alternative routes the drivers can take. Once we took a ride from a milkman. We were somewhere in Kedah, I think. David and I had just been dropped off by a driver who was not going where we wanted to go. The problem was we did not realise the milkman was enroute to delivering milk to the village, so we ended up going on a slow and long detour, only to get off where we had gotten on!

That maiden hitchhiking trip to Malaysia probably triggered the wanderlust in me. I still love to travel, but I no longer travel like that. In those days, we didn't think much, if at all, about danger. Malaysia was then a very safe place. We had nothing to lose – we were young and relatively poor. In fact we had to convince the drivers we were not dangerous, and that we were after nothing but a ride. In my mind,

David Low (second from right) and me (extreme right), on our hitchhiking trip to Pulau Langkawi after our O-levels, 1966.

Pre-University 2 class in Tanjong Katong Secondary School, 1968. We were the first batch of Pre-U students at the time. I'm in the middle row, second from the left.

this trip represents a nostalgic and charming recollection of a simpler time and a friendlier world.

Square peg in a round hole

When I was considering my post-secondary options, my career master in school persuaded me to do Science instead of Arts. "What can you do with Arts? You'll at most become a teacher," he said.

At that time, Tanjong Katong Secondary Technical School was just starting to offer pre-university classes, and it was designated as a technical school to produce engineers and technical personnel for the developing industrial sector. Singapore was then launching its industrialisation programme, and more emphasis was given to science subjects. It did not seem like a bad idea at that time to be part of the programme. So, on my career master's persuasion, I stayed on in TK and went into the Science stream.

I was among the earliest batch of pre-university students at TK. The subjects I took were Pure Maths, Applied Maths and Physics, and Chemistry. It was quite a change for me, and more than I had bargained for. I had a lot to catch up on, especially for Chemistry and Pure Maths. Without Additional Maths or a strong base in Chemistry, going into Science was a real struggle. I remember my Chemistry teacher John Yip – who later became Director of Schools at the Ministry of Education – twisted my ear once in class because I was simply too "blur" about what was going on.

Indeed I was. I felt somewhat out of place. There were times in my pre-university days when I wondered if I should make a switch and go over to one of the other schools that offered the Arts stream. But my good friends Chandru, Narayanan and Syed Hazem persuaded me to stay on, lending me their notes at times to help me along. I would not have made it through without their help. On hindsight, the teachers should have warned me against taking up Science given my lack of foundation. Perhaps, too, I should have insisted on pursuing a more Arts-based education. But I have no regrets. Doing Science at pre-university level stretched my mind. I had to learn from my classmates who were stronger, and work on my weaker subjects. I graduated with results good enough to go on to university.

And it was in university that I had my awakening.

Chapter 2

UNIVERSITY AND SOME OF THE BEST TIMES OF MY LIFE

MY FIRST TRIP to the University of Singapore in 1969 was something of a shock. I had gone to the campus, which was then at Bukit Timah, with my good friend Chandru. We were walking past the Union House canteen towards the admissions office to sort out some administrative details when we were waylaid by some raggers. They were a group of seniors hanging out at the canteen. "Freshies, come here!" they shouted to us. We said we were not freshmen, to which one of them shot back, "As long as you're on campus, you're a freshie."

They made us sit down with them and asked us all sorts of questions – what were our names, where were we from and so on. They tried to make us do chores for them such as buying food and drinks, and serve it to them. I had heard about ragging at the university from some friends, so I was expecting it but it still came as a shock. I was trying to adapt to the situation. But Chandru was more principled: "Why should I do things for you? Who are you? I don't know who you are." The king ragger was outraged that Chandru retorted and challenged him. I intervened and signalled to Chandru to play along. After about half an hour of ragging us, they let us go.

I learned, from that day, to play along during the ragging instead of fighting it. If we fought it, we'd have gotten a harder time. Ragging was so much a part of university orientation, especially back in those days. Even the ladies would rag the freshmen. But generally, the ragging game was nothing extreme. It was more of a tease, where the seniors would make the freshmen answer questions and run errands and the like. It was all in good fun although there was an episode which marred the orientation ragging.

It was the case of Marianne Jansen. Like most freshmen, Marianne Jansen was ragged. Like me the year before, she had come onto the campus before the term started to sort out some administrative details. A few of my friends stopped her and started asking her questions, including about her racial origins. As a Eurasian, Marianne indicated that she had her roots in various racial groups. One ragger asked if she had Indian blood, to which she answered no. Then she was asked if she wanted some Indian blood. That was construed as sexually insinuating. She reported the incident to her parents, and her father, Professor J.A. Jansen of the Faculty of Dentistry, complained to the university. A committee of inquiry was convened and three of the raggers were charged and suspended from university for a few weeks.

While that put a dampener on ragging games for a while, it did not eradicate them. In recent years, however, with some activities taken to extreme, the university has banned "negative activities" during freshmen orientation camps and activities. The challenge for everyone now is to see how orientation programmes can be positive and facilitate interaction among students from different faculties and years. The ultimate aim must be to build a vibrant university community.

*　*　*

I had come to the university by a slight detour.

After my A-levels, I applied for and received a scholarship to do a degree in Nautical Studies in Plymouth University in the UK. For a few months, I went to Singapore Polytechnic at Prince Edward Road to attend an induction course linked to the degree. I had signed up for the scholarship because I wanted to be a merchant sailor, which, in those days, paid well. But an eye test a short while into the induction course revealed that I did not have perfect eyesight. Even if I completed the full degree programme and passed with flying colours, I would still be assigned a desk job. That was pointless. I did not want to be desk-bound so I quit the course a couple of months in. There was no penalty for giving up the scholarship as I was still in the pre-degree induction programme.

Thankfully, the window for university applications was still open, and I managed to submit my application in time. I had enquired whether it was possible for me to switch to Law or to the Social Sciences, but my Science subjects at Cambridge A-levels meant I could only apply to the Engineering or Science faculty. I applied to the latter and was accepted.

I threw myself into university life. In my first year, I participated in many orientation activities. I also attended the many tea parties and events that various societies hosted to attract new members. At these gatherings and events, I got to meet people from different parts of Singapore and from different faculties. Many of them were very nice, and I made friends with some of them. These friendships helped me through university, especially when I was active in the Student Union. Participation made me feel a part of the community, and many of the friends I made in university remain to this day.

University was my awakening of sorts. Until then, I was still more comfortable being in my own world and doing my own thing. I was relatively introverted. But in university, I became more involved in the world out there. As a freshman, I helped the seniors with orientation programmes, and in my second year, I was in the main Freshmen Orientation Committee (FOC) led by Tan Soo Khoon, who would later go on to become Speaker of Parliament. I took on the role of organiser for Varsity Showtime, a big event at the National Theatre. That showed me what to do, how to organise events,

SINGAPORE UNDERGRAD

Vol. 3 No. 12 — Tuesday 10th June, 1969 — M.C.(P) 0419

A QUESTION OF DECORUM

by MAHBUBANI KISHORE

MR. Lee Kuan Yew committed an unfortunate act of arrogance on the night of 4th June when he physically pushed the Chairman from the rostrum to take the Chair. Undoubtedly most of the people at the forum could understand Mr. Lee Kuan Yew's impatience, it is certainly not a very pleasant experience to be harangued at a speech by a slow, emotional speaker — but that is no excuse for the use of physical force. In any such difficult situation...

Radio and T.V. — is tightly controlled; where decisions are made in secret by select committees rather than by open discussion and where the P.P.S.O. and the suitability certificate can act as strong disinducements to politicization, political opposition...

carefully avoided answering this question: he only said that he would never permit any L.S.E. situation here.

But surely student politicization does not consist only of the L.S.E. type — it can also consist in the initiation of an intelli...

The *Singapore Undergrad* newspaper, where I started as circulation manager. In the 10 June 1969 issue, Editor Kishore Mahbubani wrote a report and critical commentary on a talk that PM Lee Kuan Yew had given to University students.

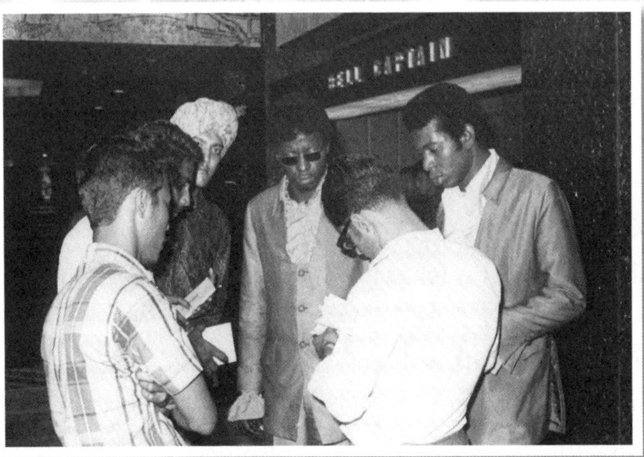

Getting autographs from members of the Pitiful Souls after their concert at the National Theatre as part of the University's freshmen orientation programme, 1970. I was Chairman of the concert organising committee, here with committee members (left to right), Yunos Rahman, Francis Fernandez and Manmohan Singh.

and I had a good committee helping me. We had to do everything from finding the entertainers to pricing the tickets and selling the tickets at schools and in public. It boosted my confidence in dealing with people. My impression of Tan Soo Khoon was that he was a capable organiser who also knew how to provide enough leeway to his team mates to exercise creativity and leadership in executing their own projects. He did not micro-manage things.

During my second year, I was elected into the Student Union and got involved in running the university publication, the *Singapore Undergrad,* first as a circulation manager, and later as Editor. The *Undergrad* was a publication produced by the University of Singapore Students Union. The editorial and operational team comprised students from different faculties. It covered a wide range of topics, including social and political issues of the day.

The day Lee Kuan Yew lost his cool with students

One of the most memorable incidents relating to the *Undergrad* during my time as a student concerned then Prime Minister Lee Kuan Yew and *Undergrad*'s Editor Kishore Mahbubani. The student union had invited Mr Lee to give a talk to the student body on 4 June 1969. As expected, it was a big event; the largest lecture theatre available on campus was booked, and it was packed to the brim. Students, and some lecturers, were sitting and standing in every available inch of space. Mr Lee arrived on time and seemed a little tense. That was understandable. Our closest neighbour, Malaysia, had just experienced the May 13, 1969 racial riots following a general election. Singapore was still adjusting to its exit from the Federation of Malaysia in August 1965 and the withdrawal of the British armed forces which started in phases from 1967.

During the question-and-answer session, many students and even lecturers stepped up to question Mr Lee on the hot topics of the day, namely the pushing through of the Abortion Bill, the abolition of the jury system and the issue of certificates of suitability for students intending to pursue higher education in Singapore. The essence of the Abortion Bill was to allow unwanted pregnancies to be terminated more easily at a time when the Singapore population was considered to be growing too rapidly, with birthrates significantly above replacement levels. As for the jury system, it was considered ineffective to allow ordinary citizens to decide on complicated criminal cases before the courts of law. The certificate of suitability had been introduced in 1964 by the Federal government in a bid to prevent students from agitating for causes in a way that could threaten the security and stability of the country. Throughout the 1950s and early 1960s, it was well-known that the socialist clubs in some schools were very strong forces that were fighting against the idea of Singapore's merger with Malaya to form Malaysia. By the time I was applying to university, that was a done deal. The bill was passed and until the 1970s, students who wanted to apply to the University of Singapore and Singapore Polytechnic had to apply for and be given a certificate of suitability.

The question-and-answer session became heated as some questioners persisted with their queries to Mr Lee even after he gave brief answers. Eventually, Mr Lee got up, rolled up his shirt sleeves and pushed the chairman of the session – one of the student union leaders – off the rostrum. He took over the forum and lectured us firmly on how we were students studying on taxpayers' money, and we should not be telling him how to run the country and resolve its problems. He seemed exasperated with the crowd and stormed out of the hall soon after admonishing us.

Of course, the outburst became the talk of the campus. Kishore Mahbubani, who was then the Editor of the *Undergrad*, reported the incident in a piece titled, "A question of decorum". In his write-up, Kishore wrote that Mr Lee "committed an unfortunate act of arrogance" by physically pushing the chairman off the rostrum, and that there was no excuse for resorting to physical force. He also questioned Mr Lee's abrupt manner in answering the questions.

The report and commentary in the *Undergrad* reflected, to a good extent, the relationship that young firebrands in the university had with the Prime Minister of the day. It was a love-hate relationship. Here was a young, talented leader who was grappling with the running of a small, independent state with few resources and friends. His style was decisive, with his two deputies – Goh Keng Swee, the economic czar, and

S Rajaratnam, the ideologue and Foreign Minister – giving him good support. But his style was abrasive, as he suffered no fools and took a tough line on anyone who stood against him. He probably saw the university student leaders as being too big for their boots.

A few days after the incident, on 13 June, Mr Lee summoned all freshmen to a talk at the National Theatre. He also met with the Union's Executive Committee and the Freshmen Orientation Committee. At the talk, he reminded the students that they were at the university for learning and education, and said he could not and would not allow organised disorder.

What happened next has never been fully disclosed. By August, Kishore had resigned as Editor, and shorn his head. It was rumoured that his scholarship was on the line, and that his resignation was not a voluntary one. It was reported that he had said it was pointless for a student to take an office if the student union was unable to provide sufficient protection for its office holders. Was Kishore's shorn head a sign of protest against his involuntary resignation? We never found out.

The supreme irony, if one could call it that, is that Kishore went on to become not only one of Singapore's pre-eminent diplomats but also Dean of the Lee Kuan Yew School of Public Policy.

When I talk to younger Singaporeans about this and other political events in my student days, they are usually quite amazed at the political fervour, courage and conviction of that generation. They tell me that, sadly, campuses have become politically sterilised since. A close friend, Steven Ooi, tells me that when he was at NUS in the mid-to-late 90s, he hardly ever heard any of his varsity mates talk about politics or heard of the union actively taking on the political establishment. According to Steven, we have reached a point where most Junior College students don't even know who their Member of Parliament is, and when you ask them what GRC (Group Representation Constituency) stands for, the most common answer is "Grass Roots Committee"!

Editing a campus newspaper; neglecting studies

I joined the *Undergrad* team as circulation manager sometime in 1969, after Kishore resigned as Editor. In my second year, I took over the editorship following a couple of acting editors. It was this time that cemented my interest in the publishing industry.

In those days, the *Undergrad* was quite candid in its publication of articles. Besides featuring articles on events around campus and campus politics, the student paper also took issue with the university administration when necessary. Once, we published an article on the issue of sexual activity among local university students. It was based on a study by the Social Studies Department. The team had framed a survey on how students viewed sex, as we wanted to explore the issue of why Singaporeans were unable to talk about sex in a non-vulgar fashion, or simply avoided it altogether. Respondents were asked questions on the concept of sexual intercourse, and what made for a sexually attractive male or female. It was quite an extensive piece. The survey showed that young people were changing in their attitudes. They were more aware of their sexuality and a rising number, though still a minority, were prepared to experiment with pre-marital sex. More women wanted to be seen as equal to their male counterparts in all relationship matters. After that piece was published, the editorial team was called up by the University Senate to explain ourselves. We were eventually let off after a nerve-wracking session where we feared for our very positions in the university. On reflection, I would say we were very bold at the time!

Sometime in late 1970, I left the *Undergrad* as Editor following an incident with another campus publication, *Pelandok*. The first President of Singapore, Yusof Ishak, passed away in November 1970. It happened during the vacation but I called my team back and we produced a special issue to pay tribute to President Yusof. The Editor of *Pelandok*, R Palakrishnan, took issue with a sentence in the obituary that was published on the *Undergrad* front page. The second paragraph of the obituary ran like this: "Born in Padang Gajah, Trong, a (where's-this-place-again?) place about 18 miles from Taiping, Perak, he early distinguished himself by getting into the Raffles Special Class."

Palakrishnan had taken offence at the "where's-this-place-again" reference, saying it was an insult to the late President. At a student council hearing on the issue, the editorial board defended the piece. We argued that the reference must be read in the context of the entire piece, which was a tribute to the late President, charting his rise from humble beginnings. At the beginning of the debate, Anwar Siraj, who was President of the student union, had taken our side. But in the final stretch, he turned on us and took the side of *Pelandok*, agreeing with them that our inclusion of that reference was "not nice", whatever that meant. When the issue was put to the vote, we lost. So the editorial team stepped down.

R Palakrishnan and Anwar Siraj have been my friends since campus days. Pala, as Palakrishnan was known, was a giant on campus, outspoken on various issues and unpredictable at times. He spoke fast and argued issues convincingly. After he graduated, he embarked on a career in criminal law and established a name for his firm, Palakrishnan and Partners. Anwar was a sound campaigner even in student days, sweeping to the position of council President in the 1970 elections. He later held important positions in various government statutory boards. As for President Yusof, he was a well-loved leader. Soft-spoken and approachable, he was accepted by Singaporeans of all races as a distinguished patron of the newly independent city-state of Singapore. It was indeed sad to lose him so soon.

* * *

The *Pelandok* episode was a personal disappointment. On hindsight, it was also a relief. By then, I was in my second year and my course work was beginning to suffer from my intense involvement in union activities.

I was doing the "PAP" combination in the Science faculty: Pure Mathematics, Applied Mathematics and Physics. There were many tutorials and laboratory sessions, but I was missing at least half of them, so much so some of my classmates and lecturers thought I had quit or switched courses! The thing about Science courses is that you cannot skip tutorials and practicals and then hope to catch up; self-study is not possible for laboratory sessions.

I tried to buckle down and study but still could not make it through the exams. I had to repeat my second year. Failure in the second year was not that uncommon among students active in the union and other voluntary activities. The university allowed one or two years to be repeated, but usually one had to pass the first year before enjoying the "honeymoon" second year. For me, it meant I had to put up with course fees and personal expenses for another year. I took up teaching in adult education classes at $10 an hour to cover my day-to-day expenses while my father kindly agreed to pay my fees.

In my third year, I spent a term at Kingsmead Hall. It was a hostel attached to the St Ignatius Church nearby. It was cheaper to rent a room there than at the university hostel, and

UNIVERSITY OF SINGAPORE STUDENTS' UNION
24th STUDENTS' COUNCIL ELECTIONS

VOTE

MANO SABNANI

Candidate No. 6

Proposer: TAN SOO KHOON

Seconder: KENNETH MOK

Experience:
1) Chairman, Varsity Showtime '70.
2) Member, Freshmen Orientation Committee, USSU, 1970.
3) Member, Editorial Board, Singapore Undergrad, 1970.
4) Hon. Gen. Secretary, Physical and Mathematical Sciences Society, 1970/71.
5) Associate Editor, USSU Handbook, 1970/71.
6) Member, N.H.O. Students' Welfare Committee, 1969/70.
7) Member, Organising Committee, USSU Annual Athletic Meet, 1969/70.

Standing for Student Council elections, 1970.

Hitchhiking in Malaysia, 1970, with (left to right) Navtej, Victor and myself – literally "on the road"! We have remained good friends for the last 47 years.

Rag and Flag Day 1971 at the University of Singapore. This was the float of the Science Society, with me (long hair) sitting on top.

At the 13th Biennial Intervarsity Games, held in Singapore, 1972, with Manmohan (extreme left), Sylvester Raj (second from left), myself (second from right), and Francis Fernandez (extreme right).

board was optional. It was in every way like the university hostel except it didn't have activities for the residents. So it did get a little boring and lonely, but it was a good time to try and focus on my studies. Still, I had to sit for a couple of re-examinations, and almost repeated my third year. I was not in my element in the Science Faculty. But I had to press on. I spent almost a year waiting for exam results and taking re-examinations. To tide myself through – I was too embarrassed to take more money from Dada by then – I continued with part-time work, which further took away time and focus from my studies.

I took quite a while in university, graduating only in 1973 with a Bachelor of Science degree. But I really enjoyed the nearly five years spent on the Bukit Timah campus. One of the spots I often hung out at was the Union House. It was a small but self-contained building with shops like Shanker Barber, and Jaabar's mamak shop, where we could buy sweets, cigarettes and all sorts of sundry goods. There were changing rooms and a canteen, and naturally, it was a hotbed of student activities. It was where many of the students hung around to chit-chat and have drinks with friends. It was a very lively place, and a place where you could meet a lot of people.

On the second level was the Union Secretariat. Here were the offices for the clerks, a small room for the *Undergrad* office, a billiard table where we could play pool, men's and ladies' lounges, and a reading room called the Lee Kong

Chian Library. Many students would sometimes spend the night in the lounge or reading room when it got too late to go home, or to save on hostel fees. You just put your stuff in a corner, and made yourself as comfortable as possible. I tried that a few times, but I didn't like the discomfort of sleeping on a small common couch in the men's lounge with other students or simply dozing off on the chair with my head resting on the table. So, I would go home for a rest even though I had stayed on late in campus.

My campus friends and I have fond memories of our university days (the University of Singapore is now known as the National University of Singapore, located on a sprawling campus in Kent Ridge). We have an active alumni group called the "Class of 72 and Friends", which has maintained close contact for the past 45 years since graduation. The advent of the internet and applications like WhatsApp has made it easy for us to talk to each other almost every day! Once a month, we meet for a chat and meal at one of the guild houses run by the National University of Singapore Society. On the first Saturday of each year, we organise a bigger lunch event that brings 60 or more old friends back on campus to reminisce about the good old times and sing the bawdy songs from our university days.

The campus in Bukit Timah was built during colonial days and was originally the Raffles College. It occupies the best part of a small hill, with buildings laid out in concentric circles at different levels of the hill. At the flattened top of the hill were the main administration and library buildings and the two quadrangles which were the focal points for student activities. It was a compact campus which facilitated interaction among students from different faculties and countries. There was a strong sense of belonging to the campus and university. The medical, engineering and architecture students were housed in smaller, separate campuses but they would often congregate in the Bukit Timah campus and participate in common activities organised by the student union and other societies. Friendships made and relationships established often flourished beyond graduation.

But for me, somewhat sadly, in 1974, it was time to be conscripted into full-time National Service in the Singapore Armed Forces.

Chapter 3

NATIONAL SERVICE AND
A CROSS-ASIA ADVENTURE

FULL-TIME National Service came as a culture shock to me. I had served in the Police Special Constabulary from the time I was 17 years old when I was still in pre-university classes at Tanjong Katong Technical Secondary School, to some time in my second year of university. The Special Constabulary was formed in 1946 to complement the main police force, and was part of the police service. As part-timers, we would serve out our commitment over a few years. We only needed to report for duty for a few hours once or twice a week.

I started out as a recruit, and together with the other recruits, we had penal code lessons, drill parades and other exercises. Usually, these activities – or shifts – took place in the evenings from 6 p.m. to 9.30 p.m. We would report to our designated centres for training or duty. We were given a token allowance and were issued with a baton and shorts. We were not armed, and most of our assignments were fairly easy and not physically demanding. Once our basic training was completed, we were sent out in pairs to patrol the surrounding residential areas to make sure that everything was in order. Later, we were required to turn in incident reports or traffic summons. Every team had to meet a loose quota. This was imposed after the authorities found out some of the patrols were off chilling in the back lanes instead of patrolling. So to prevent us from further skiving off, a quota was implemented to make sure we were really out on the streets.

I would have fulfilled my "national service" duty by the time I completed my university. Unfortunately, the Special Constabulary members who had gone to university were demobilised in the early 1970s, after the "A question of decorum" incident. There may not be a causal connection between the two events, but the fact is a new ruling required all eligible Singaporean males to do full-time NS. That meant my years in the Special Constabulary were not counted towards my National Service obligations. So like all the other eligible males, I waited to receive my call-up to NS, which came some time after I graduated from university. I was sent to Taman Jurong camp as part of the artillery team.

Being "tekanned", or bullied, was part and parcel of NS. Even the smallest thing could earn a recruit a *tekan* session. Once I had a missing button on my uniform which was spotted during inspection. As my punishment, I had to collect buttons from all my platoon mates (from their "housewife kits") and sew them all onto my green vest. I was to turn up wearing the vest at the appointed time at my corporal's room. I did not have the luxury of time to spend the day collecting and sewing the buttons as I still had to do my drills and exercises. Fortunately, a few of my mates kindly offered to help me collect and sew some of the buttons. That saved me much time and grief, and I was able to serve out my "punishment" without further incident.

On another occasion, I was pulled up by the Camp Commandant at Taman Jurong to conduct a few classes for him. We had briefly known each other in university, but were never close. But he told me this – even though I was giving the lectures on his behalf, I was by no means an officer and I just had to do what he told me to do. I was being marked for my university background. "You think you're big-time? This is the army, you're a nobody here. You do what I tell you to do, do you understand?" That was what he said to me.

Some of my more seasoned NS friends often told me: keep your head down. That, I took to heart.

After the initial three-month-long Basic Military Training (BMT), I was sent for a four-week conversion course to become an artillery mortarman in Kangaw camp, Sembawang. That proved to be a torturous period as the six of us in one 120mm mortar detachment struggled to make it. It seemed we were all chosen to be artillery mortarmen because we had science or engineering backgrounds. The idea was that science graduates would be better able to calculate the correct trajectories for the mortars. In reality, we were all relatively small-built and four out of six members of the detachment were not able to lift the mortar barrel or baseplate! So it was just poor me and another who had to alternate with the heavy stuff. The other four young men could only manage the tripod, the ammunition and the six rifles or serve as commander and just carry the board with firing instructions for the detachment.

The training at Kangaw, with its rolling hills, was tough as we were made to run up and down with the mortar and accessories. The trainers wanted to toughen us up but in practice, we were not eating properly due to long training sessions and poor or inadequate cookhouse meals. The result was gastritis and weight loss. On some days, I was surviving on chocolate and milk brought from home and hidden in my cupboard in camp. At the end of the four weeks, I was a qualified mortarman who weighed only 65kg, against the mortar baseplate weight of about 60kg!

Then it was back to SAFTI (Singapore Armed Forces Training Institute) for the section leaders' course followed by another four-week conversion to Artillery NCO (non-commissioned officer). From there, I was selected for the six-month-long SAFTI officer cadet course. On completion, I requested to be transferred to the People's Defence Force Headquarters in Beach Road. My friends said it was a nice life, and I thought there was nothing to lose in giving it a shot. Unfortunately for me, there was no position open there then and I was sent to the remote wilderness of Pulau Tekong instead. The plan for "a nice life" backfired.

On Pulau Tekong, as a young Lieutenant, I was heavily involved in training the PDF forces when they came back for

Passing out of the Section Leaders' Course in 1975;
I'm seated on the extreme left.

In the trenches – Defence Camp, Officer Cadet Course (SAFTI), 1975.
(From left) Boon Chye, myself and Patrick.

reservist training. It was a 21-day BMT refresher programme which included 5BX and fitness building, marching drills, shooting practice, defence camp and route marches. There were just two commissioned officers in Pulau Tekong Camp II – a regular, Lieutenant Tommie Goh, who was the Officer Commanding, and myself, the camp second-in-charge or 2IC. We took turns to stay overnight at the camp when training was going on. At that time, Pulau Tekong was still a rural area, with several villages or *kampongs* around the island. But many of the kampongs had been cleared of inhabitants by then, with only Kampong Salabin on the western coast still in place. Even so, the people there, too, had already received notice to move as the Ministry of Defence was planning to use the whole of the island for military training purposes.

*　*　*

In 1976, I completed my NS without any major incidents. By then I had a job offer waiting for me. I had applied to The Straits Times Press for a position after I graduated from university. At that time, Tan Sai Siong had just been put in charge of a new newspaper, which came to be known as the *Business Times*. They were recruiting. On the interview panel were Chew Ah Kong, Tan Sai Siong and Seah Chong Eu. They asked if I would be interested to join the new publication, and I said yes. By then I knew that political reporting was tricky. You couldn't really say what you had on your mind

– not in the climate of those days, as I had found out in my time with the *Undergrad*.

I was offered a position as a journalist at the *Business Times*, but just as I was to take up my position, I received my NS enlistment notice. The Straits Times Press was very understanding, and the human resource person told me that I could go back to them once I fulfilled my NS obligations, although they could not guarantee that there would be a position available then.

On completion of my NS, I did indeed go back to them, and there was a position still available. I asked if they could wait for a few more months before I started work as I wanted to take a short holiday before I started work. That short holiday turned out to be a six-month adventure across Asia and Europe.

From Singapore to London

On Chinese New Year Day in 1977, I left Singapore with $4,000. That was the start of my Asian Highway overland trek. My end destination was London – that was my dream place to be. How I got there was to be an adventure, my adventure. I was not in a hurry to reach London, so I decided I would take my time. The original plan was to travel with one of my best friends from NS, Rex Hu. We had calculated how much we needed for the trip and planned our journey. But at the last minute, he could not go as he had not raised enough funds. I was in two minds: should I continue on my own or not? In the end, I decided to, for it was a once-in-a-lifetime opportunity.

I lied to my father about my trip. Dada had wanted me to start work soon since I had finally completed my university studies and NS obligations. I told him I needed a short break before I started work, which I had secured already. I told him I was just going up to Malaysia for a week or so. He bought the story as I only brought a backpack with enough clothes and some necessities. He would not have let me go if he had known the full extent of my plans.

My first stop was Bangkok. I took a train there via Kuala Lumpur. At the Thai capital, I stayed with the brother of my friend Victor Savage, now Visiting Senior Fellow at the S Rajaratnam School of International Studies, Nanyang Technological University. I called Dada from Bangkok and told him where I was. When he asked what I was doing there, I said I had met a friend who invited me to Bangkok. Then I told him I was going to stay a little longer, maybe two weeks.

After a couple of days in Bangkok, I flew to Calcutta, India. That was the only leg of my trip I flew, as it was impossible to travel overland from Thailand through Burma (Myanmar today) to India because of the political situation then. In Calcutta, I stayed with a friend's cousin. I had a good time there. My friend's cousin was a rich man and he lived in a huge house. He gave me a room to myself. The host, whom we called Bobby, ran several shops and restaurants, and we would sometimes have meals at his various restaurants. Some days Bobby would invite me for a drink, and we'd sit in his office and knock back a few whiskies. Sometimes we'd bring the whisky home too, but we'd disguise it in Coke bottles. We'd pour out some of the original contents and top it up with whisky. Then we'd head home to the family where his elderly father, wife and brothers lived. We'd sit around and chat, and have a drink. I don't think anyone – other than Bobby and I – knew what we were drinking. To them, we were just having our "Coke".

While in Calcutta, I wrote to Dada to update him on my whereabouts. In those days, I travelled with American Express travellers' cheques. When I bought those cheques, I asked the bank for the addresses of their local offices in the various locations I was to travel to. In my subsequent letters to Dada, I gave him the onward address to the next Amex office that I'd be travelling to, so he could send me letters there. He was none too pleased when he received my first letter, which I sent from Calcutta telling him I was going to be travelling a bit beyond India.

From Calcutta, I went to Nepal by bus. Enroute to Kathmandu, I almost fell out of my seat at the first sight of the Himalayan mountains. They were unbelievable in their grandeur. For the next few weeks, I travelled through Kathmandu to Pokhara, the lake city of Nepal, and then to India. From the holy city of Benares (Varanasi), I visited the capital Delhi and the many attractions in the vicinity, including Agra and the Taj Mahal. The Sikh holy city of Amritsar, with its Golden Temple, was next. From there it was over the Indo-Pak border to Lahore, and onward to Rawalpindi, to Peshawar, Kabul, Herat, Tehran, Istanbul, Greece, Yugoslavia, Venice, Milan, Florence, Calais to Dover, and finally reaching London.

In Kathmandu, I stayed at a hostel that charged about the equivalent of S$10 a day. In the end, though, I stayed practically for free. While I was paying the bill, the receptionist took a liking to my watch. It was an old Seiko, which had been traded in by a customer when I was working at Shankar's Department Store. Seeing that the guy liked my watch, I bartered with him: the watch and a small token sum for my 10 days' accommodation.

I got the idea of bartering from a Canadian couple I had met on my travels. They told me they were travelling for free: they'd buy and sell items along the way. Barter trading in those days was quite common. Trading my Seiko watch for accommodation was one example. The Canadian guy had given me some good ideas. It was not simply a matter of buying and selling – one had to know what goods were of high value at which locations, and what would be more profitable. I remember stocking up on Gillette shaving blades, Kodak film and Johnny Walker Black Label Whisky, bringing with me as much as I could carry, but just reasonable enough to pass off for personal consumption and thus avoid trouble with customs. In Calcutta, for example, my friend Bobby pointed me to a shop that bought these foreign products. It

At the Taj Mahal, on my overland trip from Singapore to London in 1977.

At a street carnival in London, the terminus of my four-month overland trip.

was a small shop in a shopping centre. Officially, the owner was carrying on a business of selling clothes, but the mainstay of his business was buying foreign items from travellers like me. I went to him and he bought everything from me at double what I had paid for those items. He would still make a profit as he was selling them at a yet higher price. In those days, when places like India were still starved for imported goods, such barter trading was possible. Through buying and selling at various locations, I was able to stretch my funds for my travels.

I travelled mostly by bus and train throughout the Asian leg of my trip, and stayed in budget hostels in places where I did not have friends to bunk with. Travelling like this, I made many friends, many of them also hitchhiking and travelling around the world on a shoestring.

Some places were more pleasant than others. India and Nepal were great. I enjoyed myself in Kabul, where together with a group of travellers I had made friends with, we stayed in Chicken Street where all the backpackers' hostels were. The food was good and the scenery gorgeous.

I didn't have a good experience in Pakistan. Many of the local men would ask me if I was a Muslim, as if that affected their interactions with me, and I think it did. My travel mate and I were trying to get to the train station. I stopped to ask for directions. The man asked if I was Muslim and where I was from. That was natural, I thought, since we were not locals. I replied I was not Muslim and that I was from

Singapore. He gave us the directions and we went on our way. We walked for a long time but were still nowhere near the railway station. We had to ask our way around. This time, we decided to say we were Muslim if we were asked. And indeed we were. We approached another man for help and greeted him with the traditional Islamic greeting, Assalamualaikum. He asked what my name was and I put forward a Pakistani-sounding name. He started asking me about myself and if I was married. When I said no, he invited me to his house that evening to break fast with them (it was the fasting month then) and to introduce his daughter to me. I got out of it by saying I had a train to catch. That fake name became my moniker in Pakistan. Finally we were able to get to our destination without a hitch.

Another unpleasant incident took place at the train station. At Lahore, the station master told the group of us travelling together that the Pakistani trains had only one class – second class. We were reassured that the Pakistani trains were not like the Indian trains. "Our trains are very comfortable," he said. Reassured, we bought our tickets. We had the shock of our lives when the train came. It was packed to the rafters, and the commuters were blocking their side of the seats because they didn't want their side to be overcrowded, so they could lie down comfortably. No one opened the doors when the train came. We only managed to get on when we spoke to the local military garrison, who agreed to let us into their carriage. Even then, they couldn't open the door, or other people would take the chance to squeeze their way in too. We had to climb in through the window. The military guys had a good time teasing the American girls who were travelling with us. They had also "accidentally" touched the women when helping us through the window. We had to let that slide.

In the train, the guys offered one of the girls a seat. In a nanosecond a couple of the Pakistani men sat down next to her, much too close, asking her all sorts of questions – where are you from? Where are you going? She was visibly uncomfortable. I asked the men in Urdu what they were doing, and they said they were just trying to make friends. Shortly after, another guy told them that they had had fun long enough and got them to give up the seats. Then he sat down and started the whole cycle again. The few of us who were travelling together could only make sure that they did not go too far. We needed to catch the train and they had been kind enough to let us in. It was really uncomfortable and we could not sleep. We reached Rawalpindi exhausted. It was really quite an unpleasant experience.

Another time, I was on a long bus journey from Kabul to Herat at the other end of Afghanistan, where it approaches Iran. I was sitting at the back of the crowded bus. As I struggled to stay awake on the long, hot journey, I felt two strong shoulders rubbing on my sides. I sat up to notice two burly, bearded Afghans eyeing me like a morsel. Rather than panic,

I reached for the Boy Scout dagger attached to my belt and took it out of its sheath. I then made a show of using my handkerchief to wipe the blade. Turning to the Afghans, I told them in my poor Urdu language to lay off. Fortunately, they seemed to get the hint. I later got the bus conductor to find me another seat.

In Turkey, I lost US$50 through a sleight-of-hand con job. I needed Turkish lira and knew I should go to a money-changer instead of changing on the streets. But it was a Sunday and there was no moneychanger available. One guy asked if we wanted to change money – I was with a few of my friends – and he gave us a good rate. I handed over a US$50 note. He made a show of examining the note for its water-mark. I told him it was genuine and that I had got it in Singapore, so he had nothing to worry about. After he finished examining it, he said OK, he would go get the Turkish lira. He folded the US$50 note and handed it back to me before asking me to wait for him to retrieve the lira. I was wondering why he did that. I unfolded the note and saw that it was US$1 not US$50. He had swapped the note. By then, he had already moved away. I gave chase into the alleys but lost him.

In Nepal, I lost my Levi's jacket which I had left sunning on the rooftop one sunny day. When I went back for it, it was gone. I also lost a good chunk of the photos of my travels from Delhi to Istanbul because one of the customs guys put the film through the machines and they were over-exposed.

It probably happened at the border crossing from Iran to Turkey, and I discovered the loss when trying to develop the pictures in Istanbul.

I didn't spend too much time in Iran during my trip. In those days, during the times of the Shah of Iran, it was relatively expensive compared to India, Pakistan and Afghanistan. I made my way to Europe, where I hitchhiked more than I took buses and trains.

I reached London around May 1977. I spent the next month or two travelling throughout the city and other parts of the UK. To earn some pocket money, I worked as an au pair for a Gujarati family in London. My work included cleaning, doing laundry and anything else that needed to be done. The head of the family ran a shop selling Polaroid cameras and other items in the Warman Freed store in Golders Green, a Jewish area of London. I went to work at the shop too, and the sales skills I'd picked up while working during my university vacation in Shankar's Department Store – selling suits, hi-fi sets, cameras, jewellery and watches to tourists – came in very handy.

✳   ✳   ✳

Throughout my journey I would write to Dada. By then, he had given up asking when I was going home. I missed my sister's wedding, which was held in the first half of 1977. One of the first things I did when I arrived in London was to visit her – she had moved to London after her wedding. My father had given me her address but she did not know I was going to be in London, nor did she have any notice that I would turn up. When I rang the doorbell, my brother-in-law answered the door and there was a little commotion in the house when I asked for my sister. He didn't think she knew anyone in London, and she certainly did not know anyone in London. I was sporting long hair and wearing jeans, looking every bit non-Indian. Finally, my sister came to the door. With the confusion sorted, it was a happy reunion of siblings. After that I visited her quite often while I was in London.

In July 1977, I arrived back in Singapore. It had been an unforgettable adventure. I would strongly recommend young people to consider such a trip after their studies and before they embark on a career. I met with all sorts of people on the ground in different countries and saw a huge variety of landscapes and lifestyles. Obstacles had to be overcome and strangers sometimes became friends in short periods. I learnt to extract myself from difficult situations and to assist others where possible and practical. Importantly, in life you have to move towards your ultimate objectives, but without forgetting to enjoy yourself along the way.

Refreshed and rejuvenated, I was ready to start work.

Chapter 4

SELF-REALISATION IN THE BUSINESS TIMES

I STARTED WORK in the Singapore *Business Times* daily newspaper in August 1977, three and a half years after I was first interviewed.

My exposure to journalism proper had begun with my assuming the Editor position in the *Undergrad* newspaper of the University of Singapore in 1970. I enjoyed that role tremendously, even though it affected my second-year studies. The exposure made me think again about what my calling was, in terms of a career, after I finished university with a Bachelor of Science degree in Physics (and Mathematics, Pure and Applied).

I realised newspaper journalism would be an option, given my experience in the *Undergrad*. So while I cast my net for many jobs, the role of a reporter with the Straits Times Press group was a priority. That worked for me and the company was kind enough to keep a position for me while I went to do my National Service from 1974 to 1976.

Even as a student editor in the *Undergrad*, I had been made acutely aware of the constraints of political journalism in Singapore. As students, we produced a range of commentaries and news stories, not only about campus life but also about Singapore as a whole. We had a good readership, both within and outside campus. But it was not uncommon to get a reaction from the university administration whenever we published what was deemed to be a politically "sensitive" story or a rather critical commentary on some issue. The proposed abolition of the jury system in our courts; the introduction of a bill to allow for easier abortion of unwanted pregnancies; the need for a "suitability certificate" for all prospective university students: these were all running issues of the day. Even then, as students, we were called up and told that it was not for us to campaign on such issues. We were enjoying a university education on taxpayers' money and our role was to finish our studies and go on to contribute or pay back to society as good citizens in a growing economy.

So, it was not hard for me to decide on which segment of newspaper journalism I would focus on. Sub-editing involved back-room work, putting the newspaper together after the reporters had delivered their stories. On the other hand, a position as reporter in *The Straits Times* (*ST*) would mean some stories would be monitored by the authorities and their reactions would have to be respected.

I chose to be a business reporter and work with the fledgling *Business Times* (*BT*) newspaper. That proved to be a good decision and I dived quickly into reporting on companies and the stock market; the wheeling and dealing of entrepreneurs, big and small. I learnt all I could and progressed rapidly as a business journalist.

Together with a batch of new journalists, my first three months as a journalist were spent at the School of Journalism, a 12-week course run by the Straits Times Press. It was taught by Neville Krosse, a journalism veteran who had done reporting and editing in both the United Kingdom and South Africa. In his 50s at that time, he sported a beard and was seldom seen without his pipe. He appeared distinguished while at the same time displaying a gentle, almost fatherly style in his interactions with the students. He was the ideal teacher for our class of young journalists from various educational and cultural backgrounds. In those days, there was no formal journalism education in Singapore. You could apply with any educational background; if you were competent enough, it did not matter that you were not a humanities or political science student.

With me in that batch were Richard Adhikari, Elaine Koh, Peter Chia, Lee Thian Soo, Lee Kim Chew, Sit Meng Chue, Maidin Packer and Suresh Nair. For three months, we learned the ins-and-outs of journalism: reporting language, the structures of stories, what is news, sub-editing and layout. We learned how to write various types of reports, including news, features and commentaries. We also practised writing headlines and captions, selecting and cropping photos. When we were learning about the layout of a news page, we would literally cut and paste the texts and photos

School of Journalism class of 1977, with our instructor Neville Krosse (seated at centre). I'm standing, fourth from the left, and with me in this cohort were: (back row, from right) Richard Adhikari (1st), Elaine Koh (2nd), Lee Thian Soo (3rd) Sit Meng Chue (4th), Maidin Packer (5th); (front row, from right) Suresh Nair (1st), Lee Kim Chew (2nd) and Peter Chia (5th).

As a young reporter in the *Business Times*, 1978.

onto pieces of paper. Those were the days before snazzy computer programs, so we did things the old-school way.

The classes ran from 9 a.m. to 5 p.m., and there was a test at the end of the course. I was surprised that I was among the top students, as I didn't think I'd taken things very seriously. The course was useful and many of the things I learned during those 12 weeks have stayed with me until today. The camaraderie and friendships struck up among the SOJers – reporters from the different newspapers, including *The Straits Times* and *Berita Harian* – made it all the more memorable. I am still in touch with most of them today, even if only through social media!

My first posting at *BT* was the Companies Desk. I covered results, mergers, takeovers and the stock market generally. Corporate news and views was a very important segment of *BT*, it was our niche. Very quickly I was promoted to become the number two on the Companies Desk, assisting the Companies Editor. Later I was promoted to Companies Editor, and ran the desk for three years.

The Original "Hock Lock Siew"

In 1978, I started the "Hock Lock Siew" column. The column took its name from the three Chinese deities – Hock (Fortune), Lock (Prosperity), and Siew (Longevity). It was a commentary column on companies and the stock market, providing insights and analysis of what was happening in the market. The column did not carry a byline, but the "author" of the column took on the persona of an experienced market guy. Many people, including some of my colleagues, did not know who wrote the columns. Together with a couple of fellow business journalists, we produced daily commentaries on events affecting listed companies and the general market.

Reporting on companies in the 1970s and 1980s was exciting. It straddled a period of bust and boom. In the early 1980s, the market was riding an upcycle following the low point during the oil crisis of the mid-1970s. Companies were forming, merging or expanding. There were several major stories that were the talk of the town.

One of the most memorable Hock Lock Siew columns I wrote was published on 16 May 1983. It dealt with Public Bank Berhad, a Malaysian bank listed in Singapore and majority owned by Datuk Teh Hong Piow. At that time, they had run into bad debts as a consequence of aggressive expansion plans. The bank's shares were under pressure. As a business paper, we were, of course, interested in what was going on. I wrote a Hock Lock Siew column on the issue of non-disclosure, which was important given that the bank was a public bank. The Exchange and the public had asked many questions but the bank administration never gave the full story. I gave my article the title "Public Blank". It became a talking point and the bank a laughing-stock in the market. That article won the Headline of the Month award and, later, the Headline of the Year award. The selection was made by all the editors of various newspapers in the Straits Times Press, including the flagship paper *ST, New Nation, Berita Harian* and *Business Times.*

Then there was the Goodwood Park Hotel episode. It was 1978 and the group was having its AGM following a period of poor disclosure. As part of my work, I went to the AGM with questions in mind. The meeting was to be chaired by the hotel's owner Khoo Teck Puat. That particular AGM was not opened to the media; only shareholders or their proxies could attend. I arrived at the meeting venue early and had already sat myself down in a corner as they were setting up to welcome the shareholders. The company officials paid no attention to me, probably thinking I was an early-bird shareholder.

But my luck ran out. Just as the AGM was starting, one of the staff quietly approached me and asked if I was a shareholder. Apparently, someone had tipped them off about me being a reporter. I replied I was not a shareholder but was there to cover the AGM for *BT*. The staff said I could not stay as I was not a shareholder. Being somewhat petulant, I said the issue at hand was of public interest, and insisted I was staying. Eventually, they got the bouncers in and threw me out.

I reported the incident to the newsdesk on my return to *BT*. For reasons not quite known to me, the paper did not publish a story on the incident. I wrote a note on the event and another reporter was supposed to develop it, as I was the newsmaker in this instance.

I had not gone to the AGM with the intention of creating a story. I was by no means a troublemaker but I had an independent streak and when there was a story to be told, my reporter's instincts would kick in, and I would try my utmost to get the story out there.

That was the attitude the *BT* team had. It was important for the *BT*, as a young paper in the shadow of *ST*, to carve a niche for itself. We needed to have an approach that was different from what was being reported already. We thrived on exclusive stories and scoops. Covering press releases and events straight up was no big deal. We had very good journalists in *BT* who had a knack for sniffing out a good story.

Philip Yeo and EDB boycott the Business Times

One such story led the Economic Development Board (EDB) to boycott the *BT* for a few months. One of the reporters had one day spotted an advertisement placed by the EDB in one of the business magazines concerning the Sheng-Li group of companies. At that time, Sheng-Li was the holding company of the Ministry of Defence and had a varied and diverse portfolio, including defence-related companies. There had been some government rethink about the future of Sheng-Li and there was a rebranding exercise to rename the company

Singapore Technologies. One of our reporters, Jayaram Menon, wrote a straightforward piece on the rebranding exercise. We thought it was a good piece and an honest story, so we ran it.

When Philip Yeo, then EDB chairman, read the story, he blew his top and said *BT* would not be invited to any further EDB press conferences or meetings. He was angry because he said they were not ready to announce the rebranding and *BT* had scooped him and stolen EDB's thunder. We did not find out that we were boycotted by EDB until one of the reporters went to a major press conference and was refused entry. It was then that we were told we had been blacklisted.

For about three months, we had to rely on our *Berita Harian* colleagues, led by Zainul Abidin Rasheed, for information on EDB press conferences.

There was no letter to the *BT* editor or communication about what happened. As Editor of the newspaper then, I tried to set up a meeting with Philip Yeo, to no avail. I finally managed to get him on the phone. Even as I explained what had happened – that our reporters were trained to bring in their own stories and that only verified stories were published – he was furious. He said (to the effect) that we had been snooping around and gotten the stories in an underhanded manner.

Thankfully, after a few months, the episode blew over. The *BT* team was put back on EDB's invite list for conferences and events. That was an unnerving period for us; we were worried that it would become a government-wide blockage of news events. That would have made it difficult for the editorial team.

Earning recognition was not automatic. In the early years of *BT*, many of the government agencies would still go to the *ST* for their economic and company news, and they'd forget to tell *BT* or put *BT* on their communications list. So we also had to learn to rely on our own sources. The *BT* editors would encourage the reporters to scan local and international publications to keep themselves up to date.

When we received the monthly updates from the Registry of Companies (now ACRA), our reporters would go through them to see if there were any new companies that were formed or merged. Anything unusual was flagged and they'd see if there was a story in that. In *BT*, one of the criteria for a story to make it to the front page was exclusivity – it needed to be a story that *ST* did not have. We had good journalists, such as Lee Han Shih and later, Conrad Raj, who were very good with scoops. The frequency with which reporters could bring in exclusive stories was one of the criteria for assessment, which also included writing skill, speed and accuracy, resourcefulness, and the ability to write commentaries.

Our young reporters were trained by senior journalists like Han Shih and John Lim into newshounds to sniff out stories that other publications did not have. Or if we were covering the same story, it had to have much better content than press conference information. That, and commentaries like the Hock Lock Siew columns, were what made *BT* stand out.

Businessman of the Year Award

Work in *BT* was not all reporting and editing. We had a lot of "Extracurricular Activities" (ECAs) as well. These included organising and working on projects with the Community Chest, the Annual Report Award, Committee for Family (national level), Singapore Press Club, and the Businessman of the Year Award.

The Businessman of the Year (BOY) Award was an interesting project. Today, it continues as the Singapore Business Awards. The BOY Award was started in 1986. At that time, we had wanted to have an event to put *BT* on the Singapore media map. Since *BT* was a business paper, it was only natural that the event was connected to Singapore business. When the senior management approved the BOY Award project, the hard graft started. We had to organise the details of the scheme, including working out the selection criteria, invite judges onto the panel, and plan the dinner, from event logistics to menu to inviting the guest of honour.

The most pressing matter was to secure a sponsor for the event. I have a former colleague from SOJ, Sit Meng Chue, to thank for that. She had left the media and was working for a public relations company. We were having lunch one day when I mentioned the plan to start the award, which was hampered by lack of funds. One of Meng Chue's clients was the international courier company, DHL, which was up and coming in those days. To cut a long story short, she set up the meeting, and DHL came in as our sponsor for the BOY event with $50,000 per annum to cover the costs.

For the event, held in February 1986, then First Deputy Prime Minister Goh Chok Tong was our guest of honour at the gala dinner at Shangri-La Hotel. The inaugural winner was Michael Fam, then chairman of Fraser & Neave.

Despite being involved in the planning of the event for almost a year, I was not at the event. By then, I was almost halfway into my three-month Press Fellowship at Wolfson College in Cambridge University, UK.

*   *   *

The Press Club was another one of my ECAs. I had joined it as a member when I first entered journalism. By the time I became Managing Editor, I had become more active, being involved as the Club's vice president. One of my major projects as vice president was raising funds to build a club house. Using my contacts, I raised about a million dollars for the building fund. Unfortunately, the club house was never set up. We had found a suitable place but the committee was hesitant to commit the funds. It was worried about how the Club would be able to finance the rest of the loan and the operations of the club house.

For about five to six years, we used the upper floor of the Front Page pub near the Singapore River as our club house. The Front Page was started and owned by a former *BT* journalist, Peter Wong. Peter offered the Press Club the space above the pub – which was his personal space – when we needed. We held many meetings and events there. Each time we were there, we would order food and drinks from Peter. That became our de facto club house.

It was unfortunate that the Press Club did not proceed with the club house idea. But it is understandable. We needed a critical mass in the number of members before a club house could be run viably. The other way was to run it like the Front Page pub – open it to the public, and use the revenues to fund its operations. There was the possibility of either operating it ourselves or renting it out to third parties, for instance. But these ideas did not float. The money raised for the club house is still with the Press Club and has grown over time with interest earned and compounded. It provides the club with a strong base for its activities.

Travels with Mr Lee Kuan Yew

One of the things I was assigned to do as Deputy Editor was to travel with then Prime Minister Lee Kuan Yew on his overseas trips in the 1980s. In those days, each newspaper would send a representative to travel with Mr Lee to cover the stories. We would follow the itinerary that was set out.

In the mid 1980s, I went with Mr Lee on his trips to Brunei, Indonesia, Japan, China and the US. These trips were not pleasure trips for us. We had tight deadlines to file our stories, bearing in mind that time was needed to edit, lay out and approve the stories before they went to print. Sometimes, we were on the move, or there'd be a dinner event. We'd have to manage our time down to the second.

In those days, filing stories from overseas was a laborious and painful process. The logistics were stressful. We'd bring our own typewriters along and send our stories back to the newsroom by telex. Telex was then the widely accepted way of transferring messages internationally, especially between organisations. Once we drafted our stories, we would have to locate a teleprinter, usually at the hotel business office or a local post office. Sometimes, we had to contend with the public queues for the telex machines too. And then we had to wait by the machines for a while to check the telex before it got sent. It was painstaking. Later, when fax machines became popular, we sent our stories by fax.

The process was made even more painful when we were travelling in different time zones. I remember the US trip was a nightmare. We barely had enough time to sleep. The reporters would all be working when people back in Singapore were sleeping. We could not stay long for the organised dinners, definitely not for dessert. We would go back to the hotel as soon as the speeches were done and file the stories. Sometimes, if we were lucky, the event organiser would have

Covering PM Lee's meeting with Deng Xiaoping on a trip to China, September 1985, in my capacity as *BT*'s Deputy Editor.

In Japan, 1986, with Guntor Sadali (*Berita Harian* Editor), Barry Desker (Singapore's Ambassador to Indonesia), Peter Lim (Chief *ST* Editor), and James Foo (MCI Press Section Chief).

Photo I took of PM Lee Kuan Yew with US President Ronald Reagan, Washington, D.C., October 1985.

On a three-month Press Fellowship at Wolfson College in Cambridge University, 1986. Dinner with Press Fellows Mugambe from Kenya (extreme left) and Alan John from Singapore (third from left), together with Alan's wife Hedwig Alfred (second from left), and my wife Nisha.

a separate room for the journalists to write and file their stories. By the time we were done with our work and had dispatched our stories in time for publication, we were left with just a couple of hours of sleep time before we had to wake up and start the day all over again. We were always rushing to meet deadlines to file our stories and follow the travel schedule.

Mr Lee was very business-like. He was usually official in his approach and had no time for small talk. On the trips he would often be at the front of the pack with the hosts, while the journalists would be in the entourage together with his staff and the other ministers who were also on the trip. We usually got fairly close to the ministers, like S Rajaratnam and Dr Tony Tan, and often had chit-chats with them as we moved along with the entourage.

I recall an incident while with Mr Lee in Japan in October 1986. We had had a long day in Tokyo and retired to the state guest house provided by the Japanese government. Late in the evening, while we were still writing and dispatching our stories, a message came from James Fu, PM Lee's press secretary. There was to be a press conference for local journalists at 8 a.m. the next morning. We did not get to bed until 2 a.m. as I was also helping Peter Lim, Editor-in-Chief of English/Malay newspapers at Singapore Press Holdings (SPH), with his stories for *ST*.

Most of the local journalists managed to make it to the morning meeting with Mr Lee. However, Mr S Rajaratnam and Dr Tony Tan, who were in the entourage, were not present. Peter Lim was late. Mr Lee seemed in a picky mood that morning. First, he complained to James Fu about not having seen his morning glass of water. It turned out that the water was placed on another table nearby. Then he asked about Peter's absence. I and another journalist ventured that he had worked late and would be on the way. Then Mr Lee turned to James Fu and asked, "Where is Tony, and what about Raja?" or words to that effect. James Fu sheepishly replied that he did not realise Mr Lee wanted them present. To which Mr Lee remarked, showing irritation, "Are they here on holiday? Never mind then, we will carry on!"

And so started a stressful press conference and another day in Japan. The journalists were updated on meetings with Japanese leaders and new initiatives in bilateral cooperation.

In October 1985, I was in the official delegation to the US to learn more about the Research Triangle set up between the three hub cities of Durham, Raleigh and Chapel Hill. We had arrived in North Carolina and were settling into our hotel rooms. The journalists met in the lobby, intending to have a quick dinner and then get down to work on our stories for the day. We bumped into the general manager of the hotel. He looked rather tense, so we asked him what the matter was. Just then, a truck arrived and workers started wheeling in what looked like crates of bottled water. We asked the GM who or what the water was for. He told us his staff had been frantically searching the area around the hotel for bottled still water "as it was requested by your Prime Minister and his family". The Americans usually drink aerated mineral water and so it was not easy to find still water. The manager asked us, teasingly, whether someone was going to bathe in the mineral water, given the quantity requested!

In an extensive tour of China in September 1985, covering 13 cities in 18 days, one of the places we visited was the Temple of Heaven in Beijing. The temple was originally built in 1420 during the Ming Dynasty and in Confucian style. Mr Lee strode ahead of the rest of the delegation and was briskly moving up the steps of the temple when a Chinese translator, rushing to keep up, remarked whether Mr Lee was in a hurry to meet Confucius and, possibly, exchange wisdoms! I laughed, but of course I could not report that exchange.

At the end of each trip, Mr Lee would have a round-up dinner with Singapore journalists. At these dinners, there was rarely small talk, but Mr Lee would often give us very good insights about the trip that had just concluded, or his takes on international developments.

While in Indonesia in April 1985, Mr Lee appeared visibly distressed at the closing dinner. He was thinking aloud when he asked why the family of President Suharto had to amass so much wealth. It seemed the man himself was clean but his family members were milking his connections and there seemed no end to it. Some members wanted a share of almost every large project! But then, Mr Lee also showed his soft side. The dinners would usually feature less meat and more fruits and vegetables. I recall how he offered the small group of journalists large slices of rock melon and none of us dared to refuse even though we had had enough fruit. "It is good for you!" he remarked.

It was always insightful and stressful travelling with Mr Lee. We had to be on our toes at all times, and it was not beyond him to give a delegation member a shelling if they didn't get things right, the ministers included.

To this day, I still keep the briefcases I used on these overseas trips with Mr Lee. They are good reminders of the experiences and my time as Deputy Editor.

Making Business Times a must-read newspaper

The trips with Mr Lee also signalled how *BT* was transforming itself into a comprehensive paper, and how the government and other newsmakers were regarding *BT*. Our paper was initially not on the PM's media invite list, perhaps because we were still a small paper and our focus was on business rather than politics. From the perspective of the editorial team, most of the stories generated from the trips would not be exclusives – one of the main features of *BT* – and we could have picked them up from either the *Straits Times* or *Berita Harian*.

But there had been a rethink in *BT*. To make it worthwhile for people to buy *BT*, we had to ask ourselves whether readers could get by with just reading the *BT* and not any other newspaper. We needed *BT* to be self-contained and complete as a Singapore daily morning newspaper.

In the early days, people doubted that *BT* would work out in the long run or survive. It had started as a thrice-weekly supplement in the *Straits Times* before it was launched in October 1976 as a full-fledged newspaper. Tan Sai Siong was the founding Editor. The newspaper, which started with 12 pages, was staffed by a small team of 30 to 40 people, including reporters, sub-editors, advertising, and support staff.

By the 1980s, *BT* had found its footing as a niche business newspaper and was gaining some recognition. But it was still hardly profitable. How to make the newspaper profitable and increase our circulation was the key to the paper's sustainability. We needed to push the paper to another level. At *BT*, the team felt that the paper must be self-contained and complete even if our strength was in business. Our model was the *Financial Times*, which we considered the best newspaper. We wanted *BT* to move in that direction, so we began to cover parliamentary sessions. While we did not have a political desk, we moved some reporters to cover politics.

We started a section called Executive Lifestyle covering high-end leisure, which included the personal investment section, talking about collecting, stocks, bonds, and property. This was especially crucial in bringing our Saturday edition from the lowest circulation issue to one of our best-selling ones. In the 1980s, many companies were moving towards a five-day work week. While the Saturday papers

The *Business Times* newsroom on the fifth floor of
Times House, Kim Seng Road, 1992.

The Editorial Team in 1992, when I was Editor-in-Chief.
A happy, cohesive group of more than 100 journalists and
support staff determined to take *BT* forward.

were delivered, they were often left unread until Monday when the executives came back to the office. We needed to do something to arrest the declining Saturday circulation. Executive Lifestyle added a more personal touch, and our Saturday edition became more of a newsstand sales paper rather than just an office newspaper.

Our sales team worked hard, and the slog paid off. We started attracting exclusive brand advertisers such as Cycle & Carriage, Patek Philippe and The Hour Glass. We also produced periodic supplements such as the annual Banking and Finance, and high-end advertorials like Watches.

One of our biggest coups came when the *Shipping Times* – which had always been in *ST* – decided to become a part of *BT*. It was a minimum of eight pages with strong advertising content. It was pressured to move to *BT* as shipowners and freight forwarders wanted to pay less for their advertisements. *BT* as a smaller, niche paper could serve them well.

It was an uphill task to establish and grow *BT*. In the 1980s, we wanted to be the spanner in the works of the *Asian Wall Street Journal* (now known as the *Wall Street Journal Asia*), which was also starting up at the same time. There was resistance from within the Straits Times Press group when *BT* wanted to expand beyond business. We were not trying to rival or beat the *ST* on political coverage but we needed to ensure there was all-round coverage on Singapore happenings in *BT*. My argument for expanding our coverage was that *BT* needed to be a complete paper. By then, we had ardent supporters, including Michael Fam, then Chairman of F&N. He told us he always read the *BT* first, first thing in the morning. He said he enjoyed it. He said he could get a glimpse of everything significant that was happening in Singapore and elsewhere.

There was always a question: was the Straits Times Press group serious about the sustainability and longevity of *BT* or was it seen merely as a block against the *Asian Wall Street Journal* having the field to itself? At that time, even though *BT* was already established as a business paper, the *Straits Times* maintained its own business news pages. Initially the section was called Times Business, which created confusion for a lot of readers and partners. They later changed it to Times Dollar. Once, a newly appointed staff member – who was to become a member of the senior management of Singapore Press Holdings – said to me at his orientation: Why should we have a separate *BT*? *BT* should just be folded into *ST*, and be made a strong business section in *ST*. I was then Editor of *BT*, and was of course taken aback. Thankfully, he was not the one calling the shots then, so nothing happened. That was the extent of resistance we had to overcome.

Later, as *BT* became more profitable and accepted by the important sectors of the business world, the Straits Times Press also began to accept that *BT* was a paper in its own right. We were always on the lookout for good writers and did a lot to nurture young reporters. Over the years, *BT* had a lot of good writers, including Margaret Thomas, Brian Gomez,

BusinessTimes

THE BUSINESS PAPER FOR S-E ASIA — READ FROM BALIKPAPAN TO BINTULU, MARUTI TO MONGKOK

MITA (P) 35/12/91 · Tuesday, April 28, 1992 · 75¢ cash or 25¢ in three painless instalments

NEWS SUMMARY

Bollywood, here he comes

BOMBAY — Starduct, the only entertainment/business paper in Bombay, the Hollywood of the East, has appointed Mano Sabnani, the former editor of BT, as its consultant. A Starduct spokesman said Mr Sabnani was highly recommended by Pamela Bordes, who is now a well-known photographer here. "Pappadum" Pam disclosed that she met Mr Sabnani while holidaying in South-east Asia. "He likes pappadum" was all she would say when asked about him.

Star trekker

KATHMANDU — Nepal has asked former BT editor Mano Sabnani for advice on how to attract more stressed-out journalists here. The government said Mr Sabnani, who went trekking these some years ago, had helped throw a trail which brought much sought-after foreign exchange to Nepal.

Pinnacle hits low

BUSINESS at the Pinnacle of OUB Centre is expected to suffer now that former BT editor Mano Sabnani will no longer be taking his contacts for lunch at the exclusive restaurant on analysts. They predict business booming at the Times House canteen where Mr Sabnani is expected to regularly lunch with colleagues who have become addicted to the food cooked by "Ah Lim". — Page 2

Mono Mano

THE karaoke craze in Singapore has helped uncover many a talent and allowed some MPs to demonstrate that they can sing. Former BT editor Mano Sabnani has discovered that he too can sing and is coming out with an LP entitled Mono Mano. — Page 8

Ee-Chee habit

FORMER BT reporter Chan Oi Chee confirmed yesterday from Hongkong that she has filed a claim against her former boss, Mano Sabnani, for disrupting her lifestyle. "I've picked up his blinking habit," she says. "Now I can't seem to get rid of it." — Page 9

Macrobiotic Mano

IS former BT editor Mano Sabnani's lifestyle healthy? All work and no play? Meeting after meeting? Is all that roast and prata giving him high cholesterol? Former BT news editor Richard Seah, currently publisher and editor of The Good Life, gives his assessment. — Page 13

SIA flying to Timbuktu

SIA is now planning to add legendary Timbuktu to its list of destinations — a move endorsed by ex-BT editor Mano Sabnani, who invested in a camel park there a few years ago. — Shipping Times Page 1

MARKET SUMMARY

Dow plunges

WALL STREET stocks fell at the opening yesterday on news that the respected editor of South-east Asia's leading business daily has decided to move on. The Dow Jones index of leading industrial shares lost 444.4 points to 1,688 in the first five minutes of trade.

Footsie plummets

LONDON shares were lower at midday yesterday amid panic selling following a report of the departure of editor Mano Sabnani from Singapore's influential business daily. At 1234 GMT, the FTSE 100-Share Index was at 2,468, down 45.94 per cent.

NY listing for Goldtron

GOLDTRON, formerly known as Gold Coin, has won approval for a listing on the New York Stock Exchange. We reprint what BT's then compensates editor Mano Sabnani, predicted in 1982 about the future of the company. — Page 3

New market index

FORMER BT editor Mano Sabnani has come up with a new market indicator, the BT-MS index. To be launched on April 1, 1993, it will keep track of all stock movements, including those on Cloth International. Those who rely on it will not be clubbered, Mr Sabnani promises. — Page 4

Fowl treatment

PRIMA is opening a fertility clinic for chickens in Ipoh as part of efforts to boost its bottom line. — Page 6

STOCK INDICES

ST INDUSTRIALS 489 (-999)

	Monday	Change
BT-MGA	+73	487.4
Kuala Lumpur	+3.45	385.7
Tokyo	17,688.99	+406.1
Hongkong	1,632.1	4,529
Sydney	482.1	+452

	Friday	Change
New York	3,169.43	+6.69
London	2,735.72	+25.3

CURRENCIES

London Gold

AM fix .... US$328.50 +US$0.65

Exchange rates

US$	S$ 1.6465
100 Yen	S$ 1.2319
M$	S$ 0.6669

Money market rates

Overnight	2¾%	1/4
3-month	3 5/16%	unch

COMMODITIES

Rubber

Spot June	167.75¢/kg	-5.25
M'sia June	256.50¢/kg	-5.50

KL Tin

Turnover	36 tonnes	+7
Spot	M$15.10/kg	+0.17

Crude palm oil

Turnover	596 lots	-494
May	M$877.0/tonne	+7

CONTENTS

Editor leaves BT for the Straits and narrow way

Paper bids farewell to the man who put the M in manologue

Assessing assets: The ever intrepid Mr Sabnani focusing on the bare facts at a Manufacturers' shareholders' meeting

By Stuffed Reporters

SINGAPORE — In a move expected to have far-reaching consequences for Singapore journalism, BT editor Mano Sabnani is to leave the newspaper to which he has devoted 15 years of long hours.

Mr Sabnani is to swop jobs with The Straits Times managing editor Patrick Daniel.

Announcing the swop, Cheong Yip Seng, editor-in-chief of Singapore Press Holdings' English/Malay newspapers, said: "We are competing for the next lap in BT's development."

Mr Sabnani broke the news to staff yesterday. He concluded his terse five-hour speech with these words: "Well, this is it. It's time for me to go. But I leave a BT in good shape, and am confident that given good leadership, the continued commitment of good staff, and good food, the paper and its people will continue to grow."

BT staffers are still digesting the news. Analysts, however, have been quick to read a political motive to the move. Said one analyst: "I think Patrick Daniel is taking over Mano's place because the government wants BT to be more pro-government. Mano was moderate but perhaps still too liberal for the government's liking. (webe can this be right? — mano)

Others see it as an effort by Mr Cheong to bring to The Straits Times a better understanding of the business world. Said an enterprising: "The Straits Times is plagued by politics. Singaporeans want to make money; they're not looking for an insight into political matters."

Neither Mr Sabnani nor Mr Daniel would comment on these views. Speaking to reporters last night at the premiere of the latest RJ45 film, Information and the Arts Minister George Yeo said there would be no change in his "OB markers".

In his 15 years with BT, Mr Sabnani rose from cub reporter to its editor in just four years. He was well known for his exposés of corporate skullduggery. In order to gain entry to companies AGMs, he bought odd-lots in many companies and is now thought to have one of the widest portfolios among Singapore's small investors.

In 1986 Mr Sabnani became BT editor. Under his guidance, BT's daily circulation shot from 14,000 to 23,000, averaging reflection on government circles that something somewhere was leaking. The rise was also attributed to BT's widely-followed column. Hock Lock Siew. Mr Sabnani made his name as a business reporter by writing this column. He also gave his name to it, for unknown to readers, Hock Lock Siew is Mano Sabnani in Hanyu Pinyin.

● Sindu to name scholarship after Sabnani, Pg 2
● Political career ahead? Pg 2
● Admission price up again, Pg 30

MANOHARDAS P SABNANI

Born near High Street in 1950. Married with two children, both extremely adorable. Another on the way.
1974: Lieutenant, Singapore Armed Forces
1977: Joined BT as cub reporter
1980: Became paper's youngest city editor
1983: Became news editor
1986: Continued meteoric rise to become acting editor of BT and Singapore Business
1988: Became editor of BT and Singapore Business
1992: Left BT's hot seat to be managing editor of The Straits Times

Mano memories

SINGAPORE — And now, the last word on Mano Sabnani from BT-ers who say they know him better than anyone, having seen and heard from him the last many years day and night …

'How come he's here Saturdays, Sundays and public holidays?' — Angela, indignantly

'First in, last out every day, but despite his stamina, I could not get him to run in the cross-country race!' — Sheela, quietly

'He's got a little boy smile.' — Rahita, coyly

'Every night, when he takes out his tiffin carrier, you just want to go in and grab his grub.' — Amy Balan, with the lean and hungry look

'Mano? A skinflint, but deep inside, he is generous. I like to poke fun at his oblong ties. Shall miss that, and the monologues.' — Mei Yin, wistfully

'He's a softie.' — Gen, fondly

'Mano-mania!' — YangRui, quizzically

'Some say he's tightfisted. I prefer the word frugal. How many editors do you know would walk from Times House to the Mandarin Hotel for a function — in the hot afternoon sun — and back?' — Chris Tan, breathlessly

'Hello. I understand you are not going to renew your contract in Singapore Business, and Mano is a big advertiser at their first meeting. I thought I would faint.' — ex-BT'er Jeff Tsang, incredulously

'Any man who thinks he knows everything knows nothing at all — Mano Sabnani, every time I had to write a scandalous story.' — Dawn, dreamily

'He hitchhiked from Singapore to Europe!' — Arlina, excitedly

Parting shots from movers and shakers

'Mano left me with only a penny! How he was able to sniff out all the shady dealings in the Pan-El group is beyond me, just like it would take me 35,316 years to pay back M$424 million for what I did to the Malaysian and Singapore stock exchanges in 1985. All I ask of him now is, leave my wife Penny alone. I don't know how he managed to uncover the way she was misappropriating shares at Supreme Finance. Well, we've paid our dues. I know Mano was just doing his job.'

— Tan Koon Swan, former leading businessman-politician

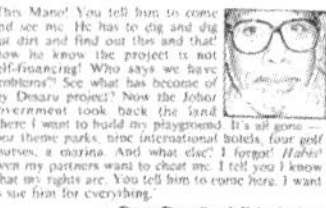

'Choy! Mano robbed me of my sunshine and allies! I don't want other people to know what I do (I have three families lor, most businessmen got many families what?). But Mano sent his karpok people after me, day and night. I had to change my longyone. Sell off my controlling stake in Sunshine Allied Investments. Move away from Singapore. I miss the sunshine, all my mahjong kaki. I went Down Under and he sent Florence Chong after me! I moved to Hongkong. First, this Foo Choy Peng, and now this Catherine Ong keeps calling me about my Allied group investments in China.'

— Lee Ming Tee, formerly of Sunshine Allied, now businessman at large

'This Mano! You tell him to come and see me. He has to dig and dig out dirt and find out this and that! How he know the project is not self-financing? Who says we have problems?! See what has become of my Desaru project? Now the Johor government took back the land where I want to build my playground. It's all gone — four theme parks, nine international hotels, four golf courses, a marina. And what else? I forget! Habis! Even my partners want to cheat me. I tell you I know what my rights are. You tell him to come here. I want to sue him for everything.'

— Thanga Thangathorai, Malaysian-born businessman who was involved in the M$2 billion Desaru resort project

— Compiled by Raquel Lim Soon Neo

News of departure sends markets reeling

SINGAPORE — The departure of financial guru Mano Sabnani from regional media giant BT shook the global financial markets yesterday, with Wall Street and Tokyo equities trading the historic plunge, each shedding more than 56 per cent in value.

In Singapore, share prices nosedived as the Straits Times Industrials Index sank below the 500-point level for the first time in history.

Main board counters Gold Coin and Prima became almost worthless after news broke that Mr Sabnani, a major shareholder in both companies, had sold his stake.

might shift his funds, believed to be worth $100 million, to new countries in the brighter Bombay Stock Exchange.

Meanwhile, in India, the rupee rose more than 2,000 basis points against the greenback within the first hour of trading on news that Mr Sabnani intended to buy into the Indian market.

Analysts said the worst was not over and the Singapore equity and currency markets might be in for the biggest slaughter ever. "We expect another Black Monday when the market opens next week," said one broker from Choo Wee Khiong Securities.

● Editorial, Pg 10

Sources said Mr Sabnani

Are you another Harish Mehta?

Can you generate 49 stories from a single five-day overseas trip?

Do you blush when a Vietnamese asks you to see the dong you're carrying?

Would you do the tinkling with Cory Aquino?

Whatever's your answer, you are the journalist we're looking for.

Write to The Editor, Business Times, 390, Kim Seng Road, Times House, S(0923)

Sabnani makes the switch, but his opinions he won't ditch

SINGAPORE — Few were surprised by the news yesterday that one of Singapore's major market gurus had announced his move from presiding to managing. That had long been rumours that Mano Sabnani would be giving up his editor's seat at BT, though the talk had been denied by both Mr Sabnani and his successor, up and coming media mogul Patrick Daniel.

As things turned out, BT's reliable sources were only off by a month in their predictions (a tolerable variance in statistical terms).

When asked why they had repeatedly denied the rumoured switch, both Mr Sabnani and Mr Daniel said they could not tell the truth until the stock exchange, which has to approve all major changes in listed companies, had been notified. Otherwise they could have been accused of insider trading of their jobs.

Analysts are divided in their assessment of the job swop and its impact. Some described it as a brilliant move hatched by Singapore Press Holdings chief honcho Lim Kim San and editorial supremo Cheong Yip Seng to pour new wine into old bottles, or should that be old wine into new bottles, in order to create greater ferment in the newsroom. A few did wonder, however, whether this ferment would yield exciting new brews or merely a lot of gas.

Others felt the swop amounted to no real change, and that the SPH bosses were merely groping in the dark for a way to break down the protective wall between the two newsrooms. Analyst Choo Wee Khiong suggested that the job swop idea was hatched in Serangoon Road by BT's most ardent supporters, its vendors.

The stock market will not, however, be totally cheered by Mr Sabnani's popular "quasi-obolgies". He will keep on giving his advice and predictions on the market, however unwanted or useless they may be, as BT's Hock Lock Siew columnist. He will go on championing Club and stocks that others have cast by the wayside, Aztec, Gold Coin, UIC, Multi-Purpose, K L Kepong, and Berjaya will remain the chips he carries on his shoulder.

Mr Sabnani is also expected to use his investment skills to raise the returns on Singapore Press Holdings' huge cash reserves. This in turn should raise staff remuneration, something Mr Sabnani was often not able to do as BT editor.

The job swop is not expected in the short term to have any effect on SPH's share price. But, analysts believe that in the longer term the price will drop sharply as Mr Daniel's lack of zeal controls and disdain for off-share issues become apparent and take a heavy toll on an already harassed and overworked editorial staff.

Stock recommendation: Sell SPH, but buy BT.

By Conrad Raj

A mock issue of the *Business Times*, done up by the paper's staff on my leaving the Editor-in-Chief position in 1992.

"Graduation" from the INSEAD Advanced Management
Programme, July 1991, with Professor Philippe Lasserre.

Past, present and future in one big BT party

With 30 years under its belt, S'pore business paper looks to a stronger product

By **DANIEL BUENAS**

IT was a party to remember, and one that BTers might still be talking about in 30 years' time.

Over 200 people — comprising staff, ex-staff, their rial products in the coming weeks," he said.

Present at the party were senior executives from Singapore Press Holdings (SPH), including Alan Chan, the group's chief executive, Cheong Yip Seng, editor-in-chief of SPH's English and Malay Newspapers Division (EMND), and Patrick Daniel, managing editor of EMND.

Also at the party were three of the four former editors of BT — Mano Sabnani, creased our circulation by about 6,000 copies."

Mr Tay also reiterated BT's pro-family policy, and thanked the "other halves" of BTers — husbands and wives — for their support and understanding.

But while the party focused on the present and the future of the paper, it was most certainly also a "blast from the past", right from the get-go.

As staff and guests arrived for cocktails, they representing each decade of the paper's life, also took their turns on stage to share their experiences, anecdotes and memories of the paper.

ers were on hand to belt out a tune or two. One song — Rod Stewart's *Have I Told You Lately* — was dedicated to their boss, BT News Editor Lilian Ang

dance floor to disco the night away. But of course, BT is never a stuffy paper, or place to work in. As Mr Tay put it: "Our in-house slogan is Serious, but fun

Party paper: *This is not a stack of The Business Times, but the cake at the 30th anniversary party of the paper at the Ritz-Carlton ballroom*

The *Business Times* marked its 30th anniversary in 2006 with a grand
party, celebrating the paper's success over the years. In the photo are
four former *BT* Chief Editors: (clockwise from left) Roy Mackie (2nd
Chief Editor), Alvin Tay (5th), Patrick Daniel (4th) and myself (3rd).
(The first Editor, Ms Tan Sai Siong, is not in the picture.)

Yang Razali Kassim, Nirmal Ghosh and Richard Seah. Sometimes, they were so good that they were poached by the more "mainstream" newspaper, the *Straits Times* itself!

*　*　*

My 15 years at the *Business Times* made me more mature as a journalist. I did a variety of jobs in various positions, and worked my way up to become Chief Editor (1986–92). I was passionate about *BT* – it was a good paper and I felt it could be profitable. By the time I left in 1992, the paper was in the black, with about $3m in annual profits. By then, the paper had expanded its content scope, new advertisers were brought in, the paper had good advertising ratios, and the readership was healthy.

At the close of my editorship of *BT*, I was looking for some change. What else could I do? From May 1992 to the close of 1995, I took on the role of Managing Editor of *The Straits Times* and Head of the Editorial Support Unit (ESU) of the English/Malay newspapers of Singapore Press Holdings (SPH). The work took me to the backend of the newsroom, dealing with management issues, people development and even systems development. As Head of the ESU, I worked with my small team on various projects that helped the editorial teams of the English and Malay newspapers when the need arose. It opened up new aspects of the newspaper business for me.

As part of my work scope, I handled legal cases for the English/Malay newspapers, It was not uncommon for newspaper reports to run into trouble with newsmakers or companies involved. Some of the cases we had to handle included those involving JB Jeyaratnam, the leader of the Workers' Party, popularly known as JBJ, and the government. One case involving JBJ went all the way up to the London courts and *ST* had to engage Clifford Chance to represent its interests as the publisher of contested reports. Our local lawyers for libel or defamation cases were Harry Elias and Partners. As Managing Editor, I was the first stop for stories that were potentially defamatory. I would seek a second opinion from our company in-house lawyers and then go on to external advisors if necessary.

My work as Head of the ESU involved developing detailed job descriptions of various editorial positions and attaching competitive values to the jobs involved. I then worked with the editors of the various newspapers to find the best people in the newsroom for those jobs. It meant journalists would be reassigned to different roles, as best suited them. We were then able to compare the performance of journalists across the board, through the different roles and newspapers, and reward them in a fair and transparent manner. The whole objective was to bring out the best in the staff and allow people to progress to their optimal level. Journalists had to feel that they had a career ahead for them. Staff turnover had to be reduced. Ultimately, such an approach benefited the whole newsroom and the different newspapers, including *ST, BT, The New Paper* and *Berita Harian* (*Tamil Murasu* was not in our fold at that time).

I was also required to solve problems involving individual staff members, including disciplinary issues and pressing personal health or financial problems which the editors had little time to attend to, given their daily grind in producing newspapers. Patience and counselling skills were needed. At times, it also meant bending the rules to accommodate and resolve hurdles faced by promising employees or prospective journalists. An example I am particularly proud of is PK Cheng or Cheng Puay Koon. She is the lady who designed the cover of this book. I sought her help after the manuscript was almost ready. I knew of her outstanding capabilities when she first applied to the *Straits Times* for a scholarship. We had scholarships for journalists, meaning reporters and sub-editors. But there were none for artists. She wanted help to finish her degree in the National University of Singapore. I brought the case up to higher management and persuaded them to offer a scholarship to PK, who went on to complete her degree and is now an outstanding and versatile artist.

The Managing Editor and ESU were the last stop for various tasks and so we took the lead in upgrading the IT systems in the newsrooms as well. Journalists were trained to adapt from a closed network of computer terminals (the Coyote System) to an open system involving IBM-compatible personal computers for reporters and editors. Artists had their Macintosh computers for graphics and illustrations.

Even though I was not dealing directly with editorial matters, I still wrote a weekly column in the *ST* business section, to keep myself in touch with writing. That work had to be done on Saturdays, when the newsroom was quiet and most journalists were having their weekend off.

At the end of 1995, a great offer from the corporate world came along, and I jumped at the chance.

Chapter 5

THE UPS AND DOWNS OF CORPORATE SINGAPORE

BY 1995, I was Managing Editor of *The Straits Times*, and had been in the newspaper business for about 18 years. I felt like I was hitting a plateau. Senior colleagues told me I'd have a job at SPH until I decided to retire, but I wasn't sure that was what I wanted. I needed something more challenging than a routine job that I could do on autopilot mode. At that time, an offer came. Tan Soo Nan, then Senior Managing Director of DBS Bank, asked me to join him at the bank. The offer was an attractive one, so I took the jump.

In 1996, I left the newsroom and joined DBS Securities as the Director of Research. There, I worked with a team of 20 analysts covering the Singapore stock market and economy. Our job was to produce reports on the best stocks, bonds and warrants for clients to invest in.

Moving into the corporate world was a change from the newsroom, but it was not that much different. In Research, we were diving deep into companies and analysing the market and economy, which was what I did in *BT* as both reporter and editor. The pace was slightly slower but the pressure just as high, if not higher, as our customers' funds were at stake.

It was interesting that research-marketing tensions were also present at the bank. The marketing department always wanted the research reports instantly, or they'd ask if we could produce a quick report on a stock that was particularly hot then. That was ostensibly going to help them in selling their stock investment or trading ideas to their clients. But the analysts would often resist, as their reputations were on the line. There were numbers to crunch and these had to be verified at various levels. It was not just about the breadth, but about depth and accuracy. Speed, though essential, was not the guiding force. It was not that much different from the editorial-marketing tensions in the newsroom.

Once, my team downgraded a call on a company from a hold to a sell, based on its performance and outlook. When the company's honcho read the report, she was furious, and the complaint went all the way up to the management at the bank, who then had to check with us what had happened. It turned out that the company was a client of the bank, and it had threatened to close its account with DBS. Eventually, the issue was resolved, but it certainly was not the last time such conflicts arose.

After a year and a half, I moved on to become Managing Director for Investments at Individual Banking, DBS. My brief was to develop investment products for the bank's many medium-to-high net worth clients. It was an exciting time.

As DBS's Managing Director for Investments, I was involved in developing investment products for the bank's medium-to-high net worth clients.

Source: The Straits Times
© Singapore Press Holdings.
Permission required for reproduction.

At Edinburgh Castle, June 1996, on a visit as Head of Research at DBS Securities to meet with UK clients.

DBS was developing new products to meet clients' needs – be it in funds or services. It was also around that time that there was discussion to merge DBS Securities with the brokerage house, Vickers Ballas. That happened in 2001.

My final position in DBS was as Managing Director for Equity Capital Markets, DBS Bank, from July 2000 to June 2001. Together with my team, we were critically involved in preparing numerous companies for a public listing and in successfully launching them on the SGX.

The five years at DBS were exciting years. I got to apply the skills and knowledge I had acquired as a journalist and editor. By then, in 2000, I was already 50 years old, and was once again beginning to think about my next steps. Coincidentally, I was also getting unhappy at the bank. There were constant changes – in direction, strategy and management – and it was getting really hard to anchor myself and my work in the environment of constant flux.

* * *

At that point in time, a friend of mine offered me an opportunity to be my own boss. He was owner of a boutique investment and equity firm, Corporate Brokers International (CBI), that was involved in buying and selling, offering advisory services and investing in small companies and startups. That was something I was already doing, even though not for myself. Joining CBI meant in some ways I could be my own boss doing what I enjoyed best, investing. Instead of analysing and producing the reports for others, I would be doing the deals myself. It was an attractive offer. So I joined CBI as a partner.

The partners at CBI came from different backgrounds, each with their own area of expertise which we could draw on. As a partner, I would find my own clients and give the parent company a share of my earnings.

During my almost two years with CBI, I had the chance to work with many startups. Some succeeded and others floundered. One of the lessons I learned in private equity was that the founder/CEO of the startup is very important. He or she is usually the major shareholder and the main force behind the venture. If he or she loses energy or gives up, the venture will usually fail. This is especially so if the enterprise is dependent on one or two persons. Ultimately, it's a matter of integrity. A company is like a sapling. As investors, we provide the money to nurture the plant. How well do you nurture the sapling? The more effort and ideas you put in, the greater the chances the sapling will survive and grow into a healthy plant with deep roots. But if the main players do not put in the effort, it becomes futile. You may water the plant well (investors) but if there's no sunlight and ventilation (say, founder's enthusiasm and hard work), the plant will die.

One such company has stuck in my memory. It was a startup by a young entrepreneur from China, and he was looking at developing a software using the XML programming language. It seemed promising at that time. A few partners, myself included, put some of our money into the enterprise. We also worked with the young chap on his business and development plans. We had regular meetings to catch up. But he took a long time in developing the software, and eventually the money was used up. During that time, he landed himself a full-time job in one of the major companies here, and said he wanted to place the company under another company in China, which did not make sense and had to be stopped. We went as far as trying to develop applications for the software, but revenues did not follow. Eventually, we lost faith in him. When I left CBI, he was still developing the software. The company is now moribund.

There were also some successes. There was a company that was converting industrial waste from ships into bricks. That was environmentally friendly and an innovation in construction. The company, which was our client, was eventually bought over by a bigger company. We made a return of four to five times from our investment.

Volatility is the nature of private equity. You may invest in 10 or 20 startups and companies, but often only a few will grow. If I may use a gardening analogy, the success or failure of the companies will depend on the gardener – the main driving force behind the company. How well does he take care of the plant, interacting with the environmental issues, such as the labour conditions and the cost-effectiveness of the products or services? That's the way it is with private equity:

you can get phenomenal returns on some investments and a 100% loss on others.

*　*　*

In 2006, I set up my own company, Rafflesia Holdings, as a vehicle for my corporate advisory work and value investing, among other things. I was 55 years old by then, and it was time to consider my "retirement" plan, and work out what I could do for myself, after a lifetime of working for others. Rafflesia would be the perfect platform for me to do what I knew best – PECAVI – Publishing/Editing, Corporate Advisory and Value Investing.

I am quite happy with the name "Rafflesia". The Rafflesia is the largest flower in the world and the official flower of the state of Sabah in Malaysia. The rare and beautiful flower grows wild in tropical jungles and flowers only about twice a year. The Rafflesia is known to have a pugnacious smell that repels unwanted attention. As a corporate entity, Rafflesia aims to be big and strong, but unattractive to predators.

The first project for Rafflesia was the writing and editing of a book for Keppel Corporation. I was approached by the group to work on a book featuring the success story of Keppel Offshore and Marine. *More Than Mettle* was written as an in-depth case study of the company. It was completed in the first half of 2007 and published at the end of the year.

Since then, I've undertaken some work for SMEs that were planning to restructure or looking at acquisitions. I would do my research, conduct workshops with the key people in the companies, and formulate a suitable approach for what the company was planning to do. One of the companies I worked with was SGX-listed Novena Holdings. I joined the company in June 2007 as an independent director. The group was then selling off its furniture arm and looking to develop a foothold in the fast-moving consumer goods sector. I later became the Executive Director (ED), helping the group look into various investments and growing other parts of the business. I left in May 2008 after helping the group lift itself to a higher level of financial performance and market value. In the following year, I took on the role of Group Managing Director for the SGX-listed Multistar Holdings. It was in the process of winding down its construction business. As Group MD, my task was to help resolve some of the issues relating to that, as well as keeping an eye out for opportunity. I was able to put Multistar on a good footing for a reverse takeover.

Gifted problem-solvers build good companies

Having dealt with companies in various capacities over the years, I've come to realise the importance of people, especially those in positions of leadership. In 2013, I completed a study of more than 30 local companies when I was adjunct professor at UniSIM, to try to suss out their success factors. In addition to my own research, I personally interviewed the leaders of these companies, usually talking to the Chief Executive Officer and the Chief Financial Officer. The information and direct quotes obtained were then combined with my own research to produce case studies on the 30-odd companies. The case studies provided me with a good understanding of how Singapore companies such as Rotary Engineering, Osim International, Kingsmen Creatives and BreadTalk came from nowhere to become sizeable groups known as SMEs (Small and Medium Enterprises), many worth hundreds of millions of dollars in market capitalisation or value.

Truth be told, there is no secret formula or even a set of formulas that made them enduring successes. One has to read the individual cases to see how they succeeded. Some emphasised their HR policies, putting people above all else. Others highlighted their ability to manage their finances and maintain a healthy balance sheet. Yet others put their focus on innovation and product development, and some took pride in their marketing abilities.

But what struck me was that the people at the helm of these successful companies were all gifted problem-solvers. Running a company means you face a set of problems each day. Some are routine and others more complex. Each problem needs to be resolved through clear thinking and be followed up with executive action. Now and then, something more major can hit the company and test the ability of management to overcome the difficulty or obstacle.

For example, say you are the CEO of a food retailing company and it emerges that the soya milk drink you are selling at your outlets is from another company and not your own product as indicated in your sales efforts. Consumers are dismayed and there is bad publicity in the press and social media. What can be done? If the follow-up rectification efforts are not convincing and comprehensive, it is likely that the company's image will be permanently damaged. This incident actually happened and the company concerned had to correct the situation and restore the confidence of their customers. They made it clear that the soya milk was supplied by a specialist in that field and custom-made for the group. Quality was high and the price charged was fair. Consumers eventually accepted the situation and sales went back to normal.

The corrective actions were thought through by top and middle management and put into action across the group with the relevant messages to the media and directly to their consumers as well. This is just a small example of problem-solving. Businessmen and corporate leaders resolve such issues on a daily basis. The same applies to leaders in any field. They have to have the ability to see the nature of the problem, take it on board and resolve the matter to the best of their abilities. Failure to do so will set the organisation back and damage its reputation and, worse, hamper its ability to forge ahead in future.

The ability to think clearly, evaluate the parameters of a problem and come up with a viable solution or solutions is the key to success for businesses and organisations. The burden of doing this usually lies with top management, which guides managers at the middle level, and it is with them that the proverbial buck stops eventually.

A good CEO can make all the difference to the long-term success of a company or organisation. Of course, the CEO can seek counsel from the board of directors or even from line managers and staff. But the final decision as to what to do in terms of strategy for a company, its values and the whole approach to business still lies with the top leader. His or her decisions can make or break the company. There is no ambiguity about that.

Besides the ability to resolve issues and problems, what-ever their nature or scope, good leaders of organisations must be true to themselves. Personal integrity is vital but even more important is how they deal with employees, cus-tomers, suppliers and even shareholders. Some companies look after their employees and customers but neglect to pay their suppliers on time. The consequence could be the suppli-ers not providing needed materials when these are urgently needed for projects or ongoing business. Good CEOs take a fair and consistent approach to all stakeholders. They ensure employees are well-trained and their performance assessed in a fair and transparent way. They take feedback from customers seriously and work to continuously improve sales and after-sales service. When something goes wrong, the recovery process is thorough and more than what the disgruntled customer expects. Shareholders and other creditors are not forgotten. They get their due payments on time and in fair proportion. Fair returns for investors will ensure the business has recourse to new capital when the need arises.

All these build up into a whole: the image or brand of the enterprise. The perception of the company or organisation in the minds of all stakeholders has to be positive, in order for progress to continue and value to be maximised. Organisations have the power to do the right thing. I call it The Power Within. Long-term success or failure lies with them, ultimately. The right leaders with correct values and ability will ensure problems are resolved as quickly as possible, operations carry on smoothly, employees feel a sense of ownership, the human potential at the organisation is truly harnessed to the maximum, and the organisation contributes as a responsible and respected part of society. Good people at the top also ensure that their values and priorities are passed down to rank and file, so that the whole organisation moves as one.

So people count in the end – people with the right values and who have intrinsic abilities to resolve problems and think creatively to push the organisation ahead of its competition and deliver the objectives it has set for itself, be it in earnings or service to the community at large.

Value investing is really hard work!

I often receive inquiries from fellow investors about which companies to invest in, what shares to buy, hold or sell. Often, I tell them that I'm not a licensed advisor and I can only say what my views are on the companies and the market. They will have to make the decision for themselves.

I was once having a chat with a friend at the Singapore Cricket Club bar, and we got into a discussion with a senior commercial airline pilot. He got quite heated during the discussion, which was about the Singapore Airlines (SIA) flight SQ006 incident. SQ006 had taxied into a closed runway for take-off in Taiwan during a thunderstorm and crashed into some construction equipment, causing the death of 83 onboard. There was debate as to whether the accident was due to pilot error. The pilot became defensive as he was involved in the training of SIA pilots and alleged the press was unnecessarily pointing fingers at the SQ006 pilots. Then, he abruptly changed the subject, looked at me and said: "I remember you." He had seen me on TV many years back when I was working at DBS, and he said he had bought some stocks (not of SIA) I had recommended. He blamed me for causing him to lose money. I told him that when I made the recommendations, they were based on the existing market conditions and outlook, as well as the companies' performance at that time. The decision to buy, sell or hold rests on the investor, and not on the analyst. The recommended stocks had done well for at least a year after my buy calls. He would have none of that. This type of irrational reaction and blame is something that happens from time to time, and I am very cautious when people approach me for "recommendations". I always tell them they have to do their own research and follow up with their own brokers.

Legendary stock trader Jesse Livermore (under the persona of Larry Livingston) was quoted as saying by Roger Lefevre in *Reminiscences of a Stock Operator*, "What [the average man] desires is to be told specifically which particular stock to buy or sell. He wants to get something for nothing. He does not wish to work. He doesn't even wish to have to think." One of the worst misconceptions about the stock market is that it is easy money – just follow the "tip" from someone and you will make money. In truth, investing is very hard work. I have friends who attend scores of AGMs every year and stay up till 2 a.m. reading up on a company, so that they can make the best investment decisions for themselves. Beware of "hot tips" from friends or even recommendations from so-called "professionals" – they often come with hidden agendas.

Riding the wave of a "hot stock" is not uncommon. But investors have to be on their toes, and if they are not careful, they can burn themselves badly. One such stock bubble that comes to mind was the Pan-Electric saga in the 1980s. Pan-Electric, or Pan-El, was a marine salvage, hotel and property group. At that time, it was a popular stock among small investors and trading houses, understandably, as its share

invest **27**

October 10, 2010 thesundaytimes

Army days led to money making ways

It was during national service that Mano Sabnani acquired an interest in investing

Lorna Tan
Senior Correspondent

Two years later, he joined MediaCorp as Today's chief executive and editor-in-chief, leaving in 2006.

For the next year, he was executive director at consumer group Novena Holdings, after which he served at Multistar Holdings as group managing director until last year. He is currently chairman and chief executive of Rafflesia Holdings, which assists SMEs with…

to university but my dad could cover only the fees, so I had to give tuition or teach in adult evening classes to cover my personal expenses.

We lived in a rented flat in Joo Chiat until 1963, when my dad managed to make a down payment on a flat in Katong.

Q How did you get interested in investing?

I got interested in stock investing during my army days. Joining BT in 1977 allowed me to develop my knowledge of financial markets and people in business. I am a value investor and agree with Warren Buffett when he says one should be greedy when others are fearful; conversely, one should be fearful when others are throwing caution to the wind. I buy stocks with good business models and governance during crisis periods, the time to sell is during euphoria in the market.

Q What property do you own?

Home is a 3,687 sq ft freehold semi-detached house in Katong. We bought it in 1998 for $1.25 mil…

Interviewed about my investment portfolio and advice for the Invest section of the *Sunday Times*, 10 October 2010.

Source: The Sunday Times © Singapore Press Holdings.

Permission required for reproduction.

Misconceptions on the CPF, the Minimum Sum Scheme and the state of our national reserves are worrying…

You know, I have been thinking long and hard. And it disturbs me.

There is so much misunderstanding and/or misinformation about our Central Provident Fund or CPF; whether the monies are safe; why CPF does not pay higher interest rates, why the Government wants the Minimum Sum Scheme and have CPF monies actually been lost by the GIC or Temasek Holdings, the two state-owned investment entities.

Well, I don't have any special inside information on GIC (Government of Singapore Investment Corporation) or Temasek or the CPF.

But from memory alone and years as a journalist covering some of these issues, I can say things are not as bad as they are made out to be.

Our citizens deserve better, and that includes those who rely only on the internet for their information needs.

So here goes. A few pointers and hard facts. Hand on heart, I think these are largely correct. And this is not a defence of any entity or the Government. Just facts!

Prime Minister Lee Hsien Loong cited an article on CPF by former Business Times editor Mano Sabnani. He shared it on his Facebook page and we reproduce it here

CPF — Fact versus Fiction

Mr Mano Sabnani is the chairman and CEO of Rafflesia Holdings. He was a former editor of the Business Times and CEO of Today newspaper. This article was first posted on his Facebook page last month.

1 CPF monies are in safe hands, no risk of loss. Interest rate paid by CPF is above market rates for FDs or fixed deposits. Go check it out. The CPF interest rate is an outlier i.e. unusually high for a zero-risk investment. As high as 5 per cent on the first $60,000 for some people.

2 The Minimum Sum Scheme (MSS) is an essential one. It should be made more flexible as planned, but it should not be abandoned. The original purpose of CPF was to provide some income in old age and that is what MSS does.

The withdrawal age has been pushed back for good reasons; overall Singaporeans are living longer and so total withdrawal at 55 years is unrealistic.

Also, vast sums of CPF money have been invested in property, and having the effect of reducing cash balances meant for retirement. Some liquidity for retirement needs has to be ensured via MSS.

3 There are those who say the CPF vaults are empty and that is why the payments back to citizens are being delayed.

This empty vault scare is total nonsense.

Our reserves per capita are one of the highest in the world with GIC, Temasek and the statutory boards all holding sizeable sums. Sums that have grown over the years.

4 Some online commentators, with due respect, don't understand how things work. CPF basically only buys special government bonds or securities, the proceeds of which are passed on to MAS (Monetary Authority of Singapore) and GIC for management. Its income is assured by returns on the special government securities that it holds.

CPF does not invest directly in the GIC portfolio or Temasek portfolio. Why? It would be too risky to do so.

But the corollary of that is that CPF cannot benefit from any windfall gains made by GIC or Temasek in certain years.

5 Another fact: Our currency has been strong all these years because our foreign debt is low and reserves are high, with relatively low inflation to boot.

Singapore Government debt, while seemingly high, is largely domestic debt. It arises mainly because of the CPF scheme to ensure forced savings for all citizens.

It's not that the Government wants to hold our money or needs it. Government is simply CUSTODIAN of our CPF savings.

6 Another fact: GIC and Temasek have done relatively well over the longer term in investments. Yes, they lost money in some investments.

But overall, over many years, they have been doing all right. Our national reserves are now probably in excess of $800 billion on a conservative, net of debt, basis.

GIC could be more transparent? I agree. That would silence its critics. But they have their reasons. Allowing citizens to know what exactly they hold and values arising could expose the country and its reserves to unnecessary scrutiny by hedge funds and other international market players. Better to be discreet; it is part of total defence.

7 The CPF Life insurance scheme is a good one. It stretches your Minimum Sum to ensure you receive monthly payouts ALL YOUR LIFE in return for relatively low premiums. All of us should take up that option, for our own sake!

Well, you have it. The basic facts. I'm sure there will be many views.

An article I wrote in 2015 about CPF was cited by PM Lee Hsien Loong, and subsequently reproduced in the *New Paper*, 12 March 2015.

price was moving up really quickly. In July 1984, there was some heavy trading and the stock's price moved from $2.16 to $3.26. It was touted as the darling of the market. While it became highly attractive for many investors, it also raised concerns that the stock was being manipulated.

In November 1985, Pan-El's creditor banks placed it under receivership as the company was reported to be having difficulty repaying debts of S$350m to 30 banks. Trading of the stock was suspended. It transpired that Pan-El stock was involved in forward contracts – agreements to buy and/or sell shares at a predetermined price in the future. In such cases, the brokerages often end up being a warehouse of sorts for the shares. The brokers' problem was that they had entered into a series of forward share deals utilising bank loans totalling about $140m. At the time the stocks of Pan-El and its subsidiaries were suspended from trading, Pan-El had incurred S$40m in operational losses. It defaulted on payment on its rescue funds, and eventually went into receivership.

The collapse of Pan-El led to a closure of both the Singapore and Kuala Lumpur stock exchanges where the shares were traded as investors were furiously trying to get rid of their shares. Broking houses that had been involved heavily in the Pan-El stocks were also severely affected. The collapse sent shockwaves across the region as share prices plummeted.

Certainly speculating and short-term trading are different from value investing, which is my main area of interest. As I get older, the need to build up my value investing increases, especially since it will be my main stream of income. When you value invest, you treat it as a business, one in which you have a stake. You look at the valuation of companies, their business models and business plans. Unlike short-term trading, where you go in big and for a short period, value investing means going in small (or big if you wish!) but for the long term. You need to identify companies that you like and that have potential.

For me, one of the key things that I look for, besides a sound business model and strong financial foundations, is integrity in the management. If I cannot trust the management to be transparent about the future of the company or the business, then it is pointless. Judgement on the integrity of management and their accounts is subjective in the final analysis. I try to get to know the management at meetings and assess them through various questions about the business and company. See how they react to shareholders' questions and how they mingle with them after the meetings. Then draw your own conclusions.

There are times when I still do a little trading, especially in an active market. But I would not go into a stock that I do not already know. Trading for me means adding to my existing position, and selling off the extra when the price is right. I keep my core position for longer. Many purist investors would criticise my approach as a *rojak* approach, but it makes sense for me, and it has worked out well.

I haven't always made money from my investments. My very first "investment" was a failure. It was around 1975. I was in the army then, and my fellow officers were talking about stocks and shares and how they were making money from it. I was getting interested in the market around that time, and I thought it would be a nice thing to be a shareholder. I bought into this company called Hytex, which was manufacturing corrugated cardboard boxes and the like. The share price was on a downward trend, and not knowing any fundamentals of investing then, I thought it would be a good time to buy. The price was bound to go back up. Or so I thought. So I bought a few lots of the shares, becoming a proud shareholder. The thrill did not last. Within a short time, the stock was suspended. Then I read reports that the company was losing money and the banks were after it. Of course, I could not recover my money.

That was a good, if painful, lesson for me. I learned not to just look at the highs and lows of a share price, and that investing entails learning more about a company. So I started to study the market in earnest, learning about company accounts, NAV (Net Asset Value), PER (Price to earnings ratio), debt-to-equity ratio and the like. My subsequent investments paid off, and I was able to make some money from them. I wasn't chasing any major stocks or hot stocks, but stocks that were solid, while underperforming. The lesson not to speculate was reinforced when I saw my dear father burn his fingers in the market. He had gotten interested in trading and was quite involved in it. I could not dissuade him as he was making a fair bit of money in the beginning. But in the end, he lost most of it.

I've been financially free or liberated since my mid-50s. That means my investments are working for me, and that I'm only using the interest and dividends earned to cover all spending by my family. Today, my investment portfolio covers a range of bonds, unit trusts and equities, mostly of Singapore-listed companies. I attend AGMs, and read their annual reports, and any other business reports related to them. My average interest/dividend yield is about 4% per annum, and the aggregate income is enough to cover our annual regular household expenses, and provide for any unforeseen expenditure. I've also built up endowment funds for my wife and our children as ballast in the event that I am no longer around to provide for them.

In 2012, I set up the Mano Sabnani Foundation Trust with the aim of promoting financial literacy, educational needs of needy children and environmental causes. It is my way of giving back to society. It is a perpetual trust and can also provide support for my family or their descendants in periods of need.

My entire portfolio of investments, covering stocks and bonds, as well as Rafflesia Holdings, are slated for the trust. The intention is that all recurrent income in the form of dividends and interest will be available for the social causes supported by the trust, as mentioned above. The capital will be grown and retained so that the trust can carry on indefinitely. I am now the settlor and executor of the trust. My role is to grow the portfolio and Rafflesia as best I can. The children can step in when they are needed.

Bright future for corporates?

Singapore is one of the best places in the world to do business. It is English-speaking and connected to various cities around the globe via a flourishing international airport and seaport. The government is business-friendly and provides assistance to small and medium enterprises, with incentives to automate and export. Tax rates are also competitive and there is good availability of skilled workers, either Singaporean or foreign.

We have a small domestic market but that is made up for by easy access to the ASEAN market and other major important markets like China and the US. Singapore has open trade agreements with many countries. It is easy to set up business, and the level of corruption in both the public and private sectors is relatively low. Local and foreign-owned banks are supportive of good businesses, and monies can also be raised via venture capital, crowdfunding and the Singapore Exchange.

So, corporate Singapore is set to do reasonably well overall. The number of successful local companies is growing steadily, and they are expanding into the region and further afield. Young people are now more prepared to be entrepreneurs and to take failure in their stride and try again. We are in for exciting times, so long as the regional and international markets are open, peaceful and growing.

One caveat on my mind is that the government may need to lift the shackles on the mainstream press in order to promote the free and open thinking needed to thrive economically in the VUCA (Volatile, Uncertain, Complex and Ambiguous) environment in this current industrial revolution that has been dubbed the Age of Disruption.

This thought was on my mind when I was approached to take on the role of consultant with *TODAY* newspaper in 2002.

Chapter 6

THE CHALLENGE OF TODAY

I RAN INTO Ernest Wong, then Group CEO of MediaCorp, at lunch one day in 2002 and we started chatting about what I had been up to. At that time, I was an Executive Director at Corporate Brokers International, focusing on nurturing and investing in small, promising companies with scalable businesses. Ernest asked if I could help to turn *TODAY* around financially.

TODAY was a commuter paper started by MediaCorp in 2000. By 2002, it had incurred a total of $40m in losses. Even though the paper was already in full swing, its advertising revenues were not enough to cover the overheads of printing and staffing. So *TODAY* became one of my clients. One of my main tasks was to help the *TODAY* marketing team connect with advertisers. Many of the more upmarket companies were unwilling to advertise with *TODAY* as they associated it with being a cheap commuter paper. Although it wasn't, that was the perception many of these brands had. In fact, even though *TODAY* was more commonly known to be a commuter paper, a large part of its print run was distributed to homes. We had to convince advertisers that *TODAY* was a quality and credible paper.

I spent two days a week in the *TODAY* office. In addition to helping the marketing department, I also conducted a course for the Channel NewsAsia and *TODAY* reporters on business journalism, and wrote a weekly column on business matters.

In 2003, Ernest told me that PN Balji, who was then Editor of the paper, wanted to retire, and asked if I would like to take over. I had known Balji from the *BT* days, and the last thing I wanted to do was to be seen as taking over his job. I spoke to Balji, who told me he had made up his mind to leave. It was then that I took up Ernest's offer to head the paper. I was made CEO and Editor-in-Chief of *TODAY*, contracted for three years.

My appointment meant I wore two hats: I was directly responsible for the financial health of the paper as well as its editorial content. It was a tall challenge. When I was interviewed by the major stakeholders of the paper – MediaCorp, SMRT and SingTel – then Singtel honcho Lee Hsien Yang, whom I had known since my *BT* days, told me that I had a last throw of the dice. They were investing another $14m into the paper through a rights issue, but should these funds run out, there would be no more coming in. Without further funds, the paper would have to close. The work was cut out for us.

There were three main areas I had to look into: editorial, circulation and advertising.

One of my first jobs was to expand the paper's editorial scope and strengthen the business desk. We aimed to provide

War on Iraq is a pre-emptive strike

SO, THE war is finally here. The media have various names for it. War in Iraq. Iraq in war. Iraq at war.

But it really is a US-led pre-emptive strike against a perceived terrorist state, Iraq. In short, it is a US strike on Iraq. It is different from the previous war involving Iraq in 1990-91.

That event, known as the Gulf War, had its origins in the invasion of Kuwait by Iraq, led by a younger Saddam Hussein. The United Nations Security Council then voted for action by coalition forces, led by the US, to liberate Kuwait. There was no directive to remove the regime of President Saddam Hussein, so the coalition forces had to be satisfied in creating no-fly zones over a defeated Iraq and a demilitarised zone between Iraq and Kuwait. George Bush senior, father of the present US President George W Bush, had to allow Saddam Hussein the dictator to run or mis-run his country for another 12 years.

The context of the action against Iraq this time around is very different. Iraq has not been on the offensive, although it is suspected of having covertly built up its military capabilities, in spite of close UN supervision. For the US, the action against Iraq could be seen as part of its extended war on terrorism and the need to reduce the threat of weapons of mass destruction being used by terrorist groups. After the horrific events of September 11, 2001 in New York, President Bush had alerted Americans to the likelihood of a long, arduous war against global terrorism on many fronts.

The priority in this war was the urgent need to find and take action against Osama Bin Laden and the Al Qaeda terrorist group, prime suspects in the September 11 attacks. That action is now history. Afghanistan, which harboured Osama, was invaded and the Taliban government of that country removed. Osama seems to have escaped but the Al Qaeda movement is at least partially crippled, with the loss of several key leaders.

Most of that action took place in the first half of last year. In the second half, the attention shifted to Iraq. The country had been under UN surveillance for more than ten years in respect of its arms build-up. The US has been deeply worried about what has been going on within the borders of Iraq, in particular, the possible build-up of chemical and biological weapons. Iraq has been less than open that the UN resolutions required and the US has moved against Baghdad, despite the absence of a UN sanction. It is an unprecedented pre-emptive strike against a perceived terrorist state, aimed at removing the present leaders.

The US has forced a change of government in Afghanistan and it will do the same in Iraq. It is a matter of time. After Iraq, it will turn its attention to North Korea, perceived as a renegade state that poses a serious threat to South Korea and Japan. The US approach is to go on the offensive to clear the world of these threats. In the process, it hopes to ensure its own security and that of its friends and allies. Pre-emptive action is the new doctrine.

Military action likely to be short and sharp

HOW WILL the US-led strike on Iraq go? It will be short and sharp. Why? Well, despite Mr Saddam's rhetoric and his regime's covert development of weapons, chemical, biological and conventional, some of mass destruction capability, he is a sitting duck in comparison with the well-known capabilities of the allied forces under US leadership. The writing on the wall suggests Mr Saddam and his regime could be history in a few weeks.

He does not have many friends, even among Middle East leaders. There is sympathy in Tunisia, Libya and Yemen. Iran and Syria dislike Mr Saddam but they are also not friendly with the US and its allies, making them basically defensive of their own interests. The Iraqi people are also not really with Mr Saddam, given his strong-handed rule over the years. In particular, the Shi'ite Muslims in the South and the Kurds in the North feel oppressed. So, when he finally goes, not many Iraqis are going to cry.

Instead, we could see cries of joy, not different from the scenes in Afghanistan after the collapse of the ultra-fundamentalist Taliban regime. For Iraq, the joy will be in the ability of individuals to speak their minds freely after so many years under a totalitarian regime. Economically, it will mean reduced military expenditure and better use of the country's rich resources for economic development. Gross Domestic Product, the total output of goods and services, is expected to improve by leaps and bounds in the post-war years.

> If the US can broker a quick settlement of the Palestinian question, then we could see the emergence of a much more stable and development-oriented Middle East. Now, that is something the world has not seen since the end of World War II nearly 60 years ago.

In short, the peace dividend will be tremendous. Effort will be needed to keep the country united on a democratic, capitalist platform. But the result will have ripple effects far beyond Iraq's borders. Its neighbours Iran, Syria, Jordan, Kuwait and Saudi Arabia will be prime beneficiaries of a stable, prosperous Iraq but the rest of the Gulf region should also see better times.

MONEY TALKS

by Mano Sabnani
mano@newstoday.com.sg

A weekly column that focuses on investment opportunities arising from market trends and corporate developments

Staying in equities will pay

SO, WHAT of the international markets? They have been like a tightly coiled spring for so long. We know full well about the economic problems of Japan and the downturn in the United States.

But a recovery is due and the suspicion is that it has been held back by the international threat of terrorism and the drawn-out standoff on Iraq and North Korea. Short-sellers and hedge funds have, for many months, been forcing down equity prices everywhere, and pushing up gold and oil prices.

But, now that the US is moving decisively to rid Iraq of Mr Saddam and his cronies, the speculators are switching strategies. They are taking profits on long positions in gold and oil and covering their short equity positions. This has been going on since Tuesday morning, when the US issued its 48-hour ultimatum to Mr Saddam and his sons to quit Iraq.

Hence, the sharp rebounds in the markets this week. There may be more upswings in global equity markets as the present Iraqi regime collapses and the US-led forces march into Baghdad.

Overall, global indices could recover 15 per cent from their recent lows by the time the war is over. For the Straits Times Index, this means a rebound from the week-ago low around 1,220 to the 1,400 level. Now is certainly not the time to bail out of equities.

At 1,220, the Singapore market was close to its September 11, 2001 low and most of the bad news was in the prices. Currently, at around 1,300, values are still attractive, especially for second liners, with dividend yields still substantially higher than bank deposit rates.

Indications are that the economic cycle in Southeast Asia is at a low end, with good prospects for an uptrend after two downturns in five years. The US will want to pump up its economy as well and that will help Southeast Asia. Continued buoyancy in India and China will also be pluses for this region.

Short war will minimise disruption to global economy

A SHORT war in Iraq means that the expected disruptions to the global economy will be minimised. We may not see deep manifestations of threats such as sustained high oil prices, rising inflation and interest rates, disruption of transport and logistics services and a lull in tourism and travel.

Instead, with the end of hostilities, the global economy could get a breath of fresh air and a chance to see what it can do in a peaceful environment.

Activity could pick up from the second quarter onwards, especially in the US and Singapore will be a beneficiary. With the first quarter flash estimate of 2.7 per cent, it should be feasible to score 3 per cent for the first half and the upper end of the 2 to 5 per cent expectation for the full year.

This is the more likely scenario to emerge from the war in Iraq. However, there are wild cards. One of the more worrying is the threat of chemical weapons being used on Kuwait and, possibly, Israel.

There could also be devastating terrorist attacks in unexpected quarters. If there are hostages, then the markets could get nervous and pull back to major support levels.

Uncertainty and fear could keep oil and commodity prices high and stock markets depressed as business activity slows down around the globe.

The weekly column I wrote for *TODAY* on business trends and investment opportunities.

STRUCTURED WARRANTS: KNOW WHAT YOU TRADE

Mano Sabnani
Editor-in-Chief/CEO
mano@newstoday.com.sg

STRUCTURED warrants are one of the hot flavours of the stock market these days.

Volumes traded in this leveraged instrument have surged, with turnover on the Singapore Exchange (SGX) amounting to $2.3 billion in the first quarter alone, compared to $1.5 billion for the whole of last year. Last month, $600 million worth of warrants changed hands, involving 2.5 billion units.

Retail investors are snapping them up, but many do not fully understand what they are getting into. Here is a rough guide on how structured warrants work and the risks that investors should be aware of when investing in these instruments.

What exactly is the nature of this instrument and how do investors as well as issuing banks deploy it in the market?

Equity warrants are derivatives that give the holders the right, but not the obligation, to subscribe to a given number of ordinary shares in the company at a predetermined exercise price within a specified time period. They can also be traded separately in the securities market.

Structured warrants are usually covered warrants which are not issued by the underlying company. They are issued by a third party, usually banks, which guarantee settlement if the warrant is exercised.

Warrants have been around on the SGX and its predecessor, The Stock Exchange of Singapore, for a long time, but the long-duration warrants issued by listed companies have been declining in popularity because liquidity has not always been good.

In contrast, covered warrants have designated market makers who are committed to quote bid and ask prices at reasonable spreads to ensure liquidity. The low pricing of warrants compared to their underlying shares makes them more accessible to small investors. Warrants also offer substantial leverage, making them attractive to speculators.

For the issuing banks, they do not work against the investors, meaning they do not win when the investors lose. But they do not work for free and they impose certain costs and margins. In other words, they provide the financial infrastructure for trading covered warrants and profit from that, while covering their risks all the time.

What accounts for the increasing popularity of structured warrants in the local market?

The underlying bull market in equities has propelled the growth of the covered warrants market this year. Warrants can do well for the holder in both a bull market and a bear market. But the Singapore market is dominated by call warrants and these are bought in anticipation of higher prices. Put warrants are not popular here.

There are now 240 warrants available for trading and they cover 40 underlying stocks. There are five active issuers, with Deutsche Bank and Macquarie Bank leading the pack.

Warrants now account for 5 per cent of all traded volume on the SGX each day, against just 1 per cent last year.

But the promoters are saying there is more potential, noting that warrants account for 15 per cent of total turnover on the Hong Kong stock exchange. Deutsche and Macquarie are stepping up efforts to educate local investors about structured warrants.

The warrants game is in full swing. What are the risks involved and what should the man in the street keep in mind?

There have been questions as to whether structured warrants are good or bad for local investors. I think there is little room for moral judgements in financial markets. In all financial instruments, there are risks and there are rewards and the two are related. High risk can yield high rewards but also big losses. If you take a low-risk approach to your investments, like keeping money in a good bank, the rewards will be very low.

Credit has to be given to the SGX and the issuing banks for building up the warrants market in Singapore with innovative approaches. One cannot fault the banks for making a good business out of servicing the speculative and hedging needs of market players. But the investors themselves have to know what they are in for when trading in structured warrants.

It is hard enough investing in stocks in the market. One has to know the company and its business and make an educated guess of its prospects, often relying on the research of stockbrokers.

Taking a position in structured warrants is even more difficult. This is because all warrants have a limited life span. Structured warrants are short-term trading instruments, typically issued for six to nine months. The price of a warrant moves with that of the underlying share and that movement can be highly unpredictable in a short period of six to nine months.

So the problem with short-term structured warrants is that they offer the prospect of high rewards, but that reward has to be harnessed in a short time period. Beyond the six or nine months, they expire and become worthless.

For the man in the street, he is probably better off buying stocks for their good value and holding on to them for future appreciation. The warrants game is really for the smart money or investors in the know.

SGX GETS TOUGH, BUT WILL IT WORK?

Mano Sabnani
Editor-in-Chief/CEO
mano@newstoday.com.sg

THE Singapore Exchange (SGX) recently announced several initiatives to enhance standards of corporate governance among listed companies.

One of the key changes relates to independent directors. Each listed company has to have two such directors on a continuous basis. For foreign companies listed here, they must also have one director or adviser or top executive who is resident in Singapore. All listed companies will have to comply with this requirement in two years' time, although many are already doing so.

Interim or half-year results are usually unaudited. The SGX now requires listed companies to state that nothing has come to the attention of the board of directors that would render the financial results to be false or misleading.

Every year, the board and the CEO of each listed company have to confirm that the internal control functions of the company are properly managed and that there are channels for reporting problems to the board and the CEO.

These measures seem to have been prompted by the China Aviation Oil (CAO) fiasco. CAO's interim results did not provide any clues to the problems ahead and the subsequent collapse was largely due to a breakdown of internal controls in respect of trading in the commodity markets.

The new requirement is that the board and the CEO have to state that they are not aware of any failure of internal controls that could have a negative effect on the company. But if we go back and take a look at the CAO scandal, it is by no means certain that this requirement would have averted the financial crisis that the jet fuel supplier is facing now. The CEO appears to have covered up the problems so well that the other directors could well be excused for not knowing the full story.

The SGX is also moving to expand the role of intermediaries in the listing process. The most important changes are designed to ensure a more transparent market and level playing field for investors, although some doubts remain about their efficacy.

Issue managers now have to help their client companies meet all the disclosure requirements for two years, instead of one. It means greater responsibility to the investing public to ensure the claims and promises made in listing prospectuses are not forgotten.

The issuer also has to ensure that the directors of a company seeking a listing here are aware of their obligations as well as the relevant laws and regulations.

These changes to the rules will help ensure that companies live up to the expectations of investors at the time of listing. Some have reported losses and severe operational problems shortly after listing. One or two have also run afoul of Singapore laws and regulations.

What is not so clear is how the SGX will enforce responsible corporate behaviour, other than suspending a company's shares or delisting the company. Such punitive measures often hurt minority shareholders more than anyone else.

The SGX also has other issues or problems to deal with, as a matter of priority.

For example, it is now studying the provisions on shareholder rights accorded by law, in respect of listed companies that are incorporated abroad. We have about 620 companies listed on the SGX, of which about 30 per cent, or 165, are foreign-incorporated. Of these foreign firms, 40 per cent are managed by Chinese nationals but incorporated in Bermuda or elsewhere. In a crisis, the rights of local shareholders are far from clear.

I think something also has to be done about the long silence over listed companies in crisis, such as Citiraya Industries and Accord Customer Care Solutions.

The SGX or the Monetary Authority of Singapore has to liaise with the Commercial Affairs Department (CAD) of the police to provide regular updates to shareholders on the affairs of the companies under investigation. The investigations by the CAD may take up to six months and shareholders cannot be left in the dark for so long.

Some pieces from the Taking Stock column I wrote for *TODAY*.

Image reproduced with permission of © MediaCorp Press.

serious, reliable and accurate content. The emphasis was on being an all-round paper. The test was this: Could readers get by with just reading *TODAY*? There was general news, politics, business, sports and features. We also emphasised generating original content, which is why it needed a good team of reporters. My senior team took a hard look at staffing and decided to weed out the deadwood. Every member had to pull his or her own weight if the paper was to work. Even though it was difficult, we had to let go of people who were simply riding along. In every job there is a need and a fit. No matter how senior you are, if the organisation can continue to function without you, you're not needed. I reshuffled some of the senior people and put them where I thought they could do their best. I also brought in writers such as the popular blogger known as Mr Brown, and got some of our senior reporters and editors to write commentary columns.

Strengthening the editorial foundation was critical if we were to attract more readers, which in turn would attract more advertisers. It was a big effort to raise the paper's profile. I had a weekly segment on CNA called "Today with Mano" in which I spoke about the business issues of the day. Philip Koh, who was then General Manager, and his team worked on improving the distribution network to include more landed property and convenience stores. How the paper was distributed was a key element for our success. The sole source of income for *TODAY* had always been advertising. Hence, our audience was tweaked to less commuters and more upmarket homes and people who had higher spending power. That may sound exclusivist, but the reality was that the survival of the paper was at stake.

We were very careful about the distribution of the 250,000 or so physical copies, given the total cost of about 60 cents per copy. People had told me how aunties and uncles were helping themselves to copies of the *TODAY* newspaper at some MRT stations. We didn't know what they were doing with the papers. Some were taking five or six copies. So one day, instead of driving, I decided to take the train to work. Near the time of distribution, I stood quietly at a corner and watched. When the papers arrived, I saw several aunties helping themselves to numerous copies. I asked one of them why she needed multiple copies. She was very defensive and retorted: "Why, cannot take ah?" I said, "Yes, you can, but I just wanted to know why you need to take so many copies." She said she was taking them for her friends in a nearby coffeeshop. I don't know if she was selling the papers at the coffeeshop or just cooking up a story.

I went back to the office and got the team together for a rethink. We decided that we could not afford to let people help themselves to the paper in a free-for-all manner. We needed to maintain some control, otherwise all the efforts we spent on producing a good paper would just go down the drain. We had no idea how many copies were actually being read and how many were being used to wrap groceries or being given to the *karang gunis* (rag-and-bone men).

So we got T-shirts printed with the *TODAY* logo, and hired people to distribute the paper at designated MRT stations. We received feedback from our distributors that some people were unhappy that they could only take one copy, but we maintained our policy. The more you restrict something, the more valuable it becomes. It was always our intention for the paper to be free and to be shared with others, but not to be wasted.

In addition to fine-tuning the distribution, Philip was also pushing for an online presence. It was a perfect strategy as we could increase our readership without incurring the extra cost of printing more physical copies. It was certainly more economical and logistically more effective. With a digital presence, people could read *TODAY* anytime, anywhere.

TODAY was a free newspaper but the emphasis has always been on being a quality paper; hence the overall cost is high. Unlike in other places, such as the UK, where there's a proliferation of free newspapers, it was a relatively new concept in Singapore at that time. The cost of producing the paper includes rental of office space, staffing, printing and distribution. We capped our print copies at 250,000 copies daily, and placed an emphasis on being available online. The advantage *TODAY* had was that the online access was not restricted by subscription, unlike the websites of some of the main newspapers.

In addition to these factors, we also had to compete with *Streats*, a free paper put out by Singapore Press Holdings.

That was a headache for us. Streats would undercut our advertising rate by as much as half and they were matching our printing numbers. Often, we would have to organise a damage-control lunch with the advertisers when they asked why *Streats* could give them a much better rate than we could. But we steadfastly refused to lower ourselves to the level of *Streats*. We set our main competitor up to be the *Straits Times*, flagship of SPH. We asked ourselves: can readers get by just reading *TODAY* and not the *ST*? That was the challenge we set ourselves.

The efforts paid off. Within a year, we overtook *The New Paper* in terms of readership. By my third year at *TODAY*, we had overtaken the Chinese daily *Lianhe Zaobao* and become the second-most-read newspaper in Singapore with over 600,000 readers, just behind the *Straits Times* with 1.2 million readers. It was a big jump from just 400,000 in 2003, when we were in fourth position. With our increased circulation, advertisers started taking us seriously. We started getting positive feedback from our advertisers that they were getting more calls as a result of placing ads with us.

The advertising revenues were key to our balancing the books. It wasn't easy to convince advertisers to place their ads with us. I'd have at least two lunches with advertisers and our marketing people every week, trying to help open doors and make connections. We had regular supporters such as FairPrice and NTUC Income. Others, we had a harder time trying to convince.

But eventually, with the mainstream media rationalisation exercise, SPH closed down *Streats*. In return, SPH got a 40% stake in *TODAY*. It was to be equivalent to what SMRT and SingTel had. All the while, MediaCorp has had 60% of *TODAY*.

*   *   *

Having to manage the editorial and financial aspects of the paper had its challenges. It was always a tense juggle. One example was the case of McDonald's. It was the biggest fast food chain in Singapore and the *TODAY* marketing team had been trying to woo them for ages. After many months, the team finally had a breakthrough, and we had a few ads coming in as part of a test of the viability of advertising with us.

At that time, McDonald's was in the midst of doing a strategic review of its organisation, working on revamping and rebranding, including rolling out cafe-style outlets, which came to be known as McCafe. It was also closing down some of its smaller and less profitable outlets. One of our reporters got hold of the story on the company's rationalisation through his own source, and we had scheduled to run the story.

When the head of the marketing team saw the story schedule, he came barging into my room and threw a fit. He raved about how it would jeopardise the ad account and how hard his team had been trying to get the fast food giant in. I calmed him down and called in the news editor. We discussed what the story was and why it was scheduled. The story had been scheduled to be our Page 1 lead as it was a scoop. Furthermore, the information was all verifiable and it was verified. There was no way we would be pulling the scoop off the schedule. I asked for a copy of the story, read it, and believed there was nothing wrong with it. The solution was a simple one. The facts were facts and there was no sensationalism involved. All that was needed was a reworking of the story angle. The story ran, and there were no serious repercussions in the end.

Such editorial-marketing tension was always there, and it was certainly more pronounced in *TODAY* than in *BT* or in the bank where I worked, since it was a free newspaper that depended entirely on advertising for its income. But I do not think I had to compromise on the principle of editorial independence. It was a matter of reviewing each case, and seeing whether the reporting was fair.

But sometimes, whether a report was fair was not up to us to decide.

TODAY at the Istana with Lee Kuan Yew

Two incidents concerning the editorial integrity of *TODAY* have stuck in my mind. One was a report on the late Mr Lee Kuan Yew's remarks on Britain's healthcare system, and the other concerned a commentary by a regular contributor to the newspaper, Mr Brown.

On 3 November 2003, *TODAY* published an article on then Senior Minister Lee Kuan Yew's account of his wife's health ordeal with the UK's National Health Service. At a community event, Mr Lee had spoken of how Mrs Lee had suffered a stroke while in London and had to go to the nearest NHS hospital as there were no private medical facilities available at the time the stroke happened. Mr Lee was reported as saying that if it hadn't been for the intervention of 10 Downing Street, Mrs Lee would not have received the medical help she needed that night. In his account, Mr Lee compared the UK's NHS system to Singapore's co-paying healthcare system, where medical attention is quick to get.

It was a Sunday when the story was filed. I was working from home and Rahul Pathak was the duty editor. We had given the go-ahead for the story to be printed as we saw it as a regular piece of reporting. After the article was published, there was an uproar in the UK over why the wife of a foreign dignitary was given preferential treatment. The Prime Minister's Office in the UK denied that it had made the call to the hospital. It was reported in *The Telegraph* that the call was put in by an official of the UK Foreign Office after the Singapore High Commission called it. According to *The Telegraph*, the Foreign Office said the reason it put a call to the hospital where Mrs Lee had been taken was that the caller from the High Commission seemed "very vexed" and the Foreign

Office needed to establish the facts. Mr Lee later issued a statement to say that he had mistakenly named 10 Downing Street as being involved in helping Mrs Lee get a CT scan at the hospital.

We were called up to the Istana to see Mr Lee – myself, Rahul, Val Chua, who wrote the story, and Ernest Wong. Mr Lee was upset. He called us into his office, in the Istana annexe, one by one. When it was my turn, he asked me if I was in the *TODAY* office that Sunday or if I knew about the story. I answered yes. He then asked if we wanted to be different from the *Straits Times*. My reply was that we were not trying to be different, and that we were just reporting what was said. I told Mr Lee we were under the impression that he wanted to convey the message that the NHS of the UK was not something Singapore should follow. That was not a new issue, and he had mentioned it several times before. To my mind, his account of his experience in the UK was an illustration of why Singapore should not adopt the free healthcare system. He asked if I had anticipated the reaction from the UK public, to which I said yes. He showed me a letter that he had written to then UK Prime Minister Tony Blair, thanking him for his help. I had no idea what he was trying to tell me. Perhaps it was that 10 Downing Street had helped but that we shouldn't have mentioned it. I did not know what the others told Mr Lee when they had their interviews.

Being summoned to meet LKY at the Istana would be, in the minds of most Singaporeans, a pretty terrifying but memorable experience. It was. Mr Lee's office was large and austere. He sat at a large rectangular table, with his press secretary on one side and his principal private secretary on the other. His style was that of a practising lawyer questioning his witnesses in a deep, stern voice. One difference was that it was not an open court and I did not know what he had asked the other "witnesses" he met that day. Was he seeking contradictions in our versions of what happened that Sunday in relation to the published story? My approach was to tell the truth as I saw it and to hope the others would do the same so that the matter could be brought to a close. In my mind, the newspaper had no special or hidden agenda in publishing the story as it appeared.

Subsequently, I had to move Val from reporting to the backend for a while. She understood why it had to be done but she also became very quiet. That was the best option at that point. She was not to blame.

I was told, much later, by someone close to Mr Lee that he was very tense during that time and that he had over-reacted on the issue.

On our part, we wanted to get to the bottom of the issue as we felt *TODAY* had done no wrong.

It appeared Val had asked Mr Lee's press secretary, Y.Y. Yeong, that Sunday whether what Mr Lee said at the event was reportable. She had a very ambivalent answer. Unfortunately, that exchange with the press secretary was not recorded by Val. But later, we found a recording by another reporter in which the press secretary was asked if the event was reportable. She did not say no. Strangely, it appeared that the *ST* reporter was told not to report what Mr Lee had said. I found that out in an email the press secretary sent to me, asking why we reported what we did. The exchange between her and the *ST* reporter was appended in the email.

We never really found out why different newspapers were given different guidelines on coverage of the event.

Mr Brown and TODAY: a partisan player in politics?

Another unpleasant incident took place in 2006 as I was finishing my three-year contract with *TODAY*.

In May that year, Singapore held its general elections. The ruling People's Action Party (PAP) won by 66.6% of the votes cast, down from 75.3% in the 2001 elections. On the night of the results, I was a panellist on a TV programme providing analysis. The first result that came in was a very safe constituency for the PAP. Although the party retained the constituency, it saw a swing of 9–10%. I then said that, all things being equal, it appeared that the electorate was swinging against the PAP. The other panellists said it was too early to tell, but I stood by my analysis. In the end, the overall results showed an almost 10% swing against the PAP. I rationalised that the high percentage vote the party received in the 2001 election was largely against the backdrop of fear arising from the September 11 attacks on the US that year and a global economic recession. Later, I was told by some people I had come across as being quite happy that the PAP had suffered a setback.

At a lunch with then Minister for Information, Communications and the Arts Dr Lee Boon Yang, *TODAY* was singled out as having given the opposition parties good coverage during the run-up to the elections. My reply was that the balanced coverage was necessary if the newspaper was to maintain its credibility. Shaun Seow, then Editor-in-Chief of MediaCorp News, was also at that lunch, but he remained relatively quiet throughout. Shaun was never involved much in the editorial side of *TODAY*. But after that meeting, he wanted me to alert him to any stories that were potentially sensitive.

One thing led to another. In June, a month or so after the general elections, *TODAY* published a column by blogger Mr Brown. He had been a regular contributor to our paper for a while. He was lamenting the fee increment for his autistic child's education, noting that all fee increments had come after the general elections.

There was a reaction from the government. K Bhavani, the Press Secretary to the Minister for Information, Communications and the Arts, wrote a letter to *TODAY* rebutting Mr Brown's column as sarcastic and distorting the truth. It labelled Mr Brown a "partisan player in politics". Bhavani's letter said: "If a columnist presents himself as a non-political observer, while exploiting his access to the mass media to undermine the Government's standing with the electorate, then he is no longer a constructive critic, but a partisan player in politics."

There was nothing in the letter that said Mr Brown's article was factually inaccurate. The letter almost felt like a vendetta against Mr Brown. I think that was partly due to his rise as a popular blogger. During the elections, he had issued a podcast parodying the James Gomez episode. Gomez was a candidate for the Workers' Party. There was an incident at the Elections Department where Gomez claimed that he had submitted his minority candidate form but the Elections Department said it didn't have the application. He threatened the Elections Department official for losing his form. Later, a CCTV clip showed Gomez put the form in his briefcase. Gomez apologised, saying he was distracted. Mr Lee Kuan Yew called Gomez a liar and then Deputy Prime Minister Wong Kan Seng said Gomez had stage-managed the incident to discredit the government and the Elections Department.

Mr Brown's podcast poked fun at the incident and was downloaded more than 30,000 times within three days. I am not sure if this contributed to the intensity of Bhavani's letter. We had to suspend the column temporarily after a discussion with the editors. Some of the commentaries on the internet made it seem like I had chickened out, that the paper had chickened out. I called Mr Brown to explain our stand and situation, that the press section had deemed him to be holding a hidden, biased political agenda and we could not host his column any longer.

Some of my editors were still fighting for Mr Brown. There were some battles that have to be fought, and some not worth fighting. Should we fight this battle? I told my team that the definition of a "partisan political player" was not ours. But if the press section had labelled Mr Brown so, we could not overturn that. Once the government define you, it's their call. The whole paper would suffer for it, if we continued with the columnist. I told my editors that I had people's jobs and livelihoods to look after. "We have come this far; it doesn't make sense to fight this battle and lose the war."

After the incident, the senior management came to see me and said there was some "covert agenda" in the newsroom. Apparently, some people did not agree with our decision about the Mr Brown issue and had put up a silent protest of sorts by wearing brown in the newsroom. I had heard about it but did not take it too seriously. Then someone tipped off the senior management. One of them came to see me a few days later and told me I had to keep control of the newsroom.

Several people left the newsroom after that.

By then, my contract was ending. Senior management told me I needed to think about leadership succession. I told them there were several people in the newsroom who could be groomed. They had been there from day one and they were good people. But the management was insistent on bringing in someone from the outside. It was not a decision I could make or influence.

I left *TODAY* in September 2006, six months after my three-year contract ended in March 2006. Commentaries swirling around the internet made my exit out to be a dramatic one, but the more accurate perspective and context is as presented here.

"Nation-building journalism" of Singapore – relevant today?

My years at the *Undergrad, BT* and *TODAY* brought into sharp focus, for me, the intertwining relationship between journalism and politics. Even a student newspaper like the *Undergrad* was not spared from being scrutinised in what it covered and how. In *BT,* after the honeymoon period where I could focus purely on business journalism, I moved to the newsdesk as the news editor. So there I was, once again covering local politics, besides business and economics.

I had to attend briefings by various ministries on issues of the day. These meetings gave us editors good insights into the workings of the government and its policies and priorities. These insights were passed on to reporters covering those beats or segments of government or the economy. They facilitated better news reports and provided the background for commentaries and editorials.

But the inside track on the government's priorities also meant we as journalists were constrained in approaching issues from fresh angles. How could you criticise a policy initiative when you had insight on its rationale and objectives? Should journalists not just build on the insights to convey to readers the purpose and benefits of a policy or some change in the status quo? However, my own approach was to try and look at aspects of a policy or action that had not been fully explored. I told my journalists they could always look for hidden objectives or warn of unintended side-effects. The role of reporters was to gather different viewpoints from the reading public and to convey these back to the government via their stories. But it was important that the opinions and feedback were based on facts. The basis had to be right.

I would say that is the essence of what the government describes as "nation-building journalism". The role of the press is not as an independent force in the country, complementing the legislative, judiciary and executive arms of government. The late Mr Lee Kuan Yew's approach was that the press should assist the government in the implementing of policies and the general governance of the country.

The thinking behind this approach is that it is the government that has the mandate of the people to rule. The leaders are judged at elections as to how they have done in the intervening years between hustings. The role of the press, in this view, should be to faithfully report the government's work and policies so that the electorate is well-informed.

Taken further, nation-building journalism also means the people and the government work together for the progress of the country, with the press serving as the conduit for information and feedback. Yes, the press can convey the moderated feedback of the people, but it is not for the press or journalists to push their own views and inordinately influence the public or force the government into changes.

I think there is merit in this overall approach to the governing of a country and the role of the press. However, there has to be sufficient room for journalists to gather candid feedback from the public and question or even criticise trends or policies emanating from the public sector.

The public is becoming ever more discerning and expects this from the press. People want to read the news but they also want to know what it means for them. They want to hear the pros and cons of a policy change before they accept it. Straight reporting from government announcements and briefings is not enough for discerning readers. The expectation of the public and the approach of the government can be in conflict at times, especially when it comes to domestic political reporting and commentary. The government adopts a hands-off approach, in general, to business, foreign news, sports and lifestyle reporting. But it is ultra-sensitive to political reporting.

In my many years as a journalist and editor, with both the *Business Times* and *TODAY*, there were not a few instances where the government reacted to a news report or commentary, as outlined in the last two chapters. The typical mode would be a call from the relevant ministry or government press section, with a request or, occasionally, a demand for the paper to publish a correction or a letter in the op-ed pages. The rejoinder might or might not be justified, but editors seldom had a choice as to whether it should be published.

Then, you have the OB (Out-of-Bounds) markers for political coverage. This golfing jargon refers to topics which should be covered sensitively, given the multiracial and multicultural nature of the Singapore body politic. Most editors understand that stirring up issues relating to race, religion and language is a no-no in our little island republic. The problem is that the so-called OB markers are not spelt out and they can shift over time. Certain related topics may need to be discussed but there are no clear guidelines as to how far the newspapers can go. The final arbiter on such coverage is the government, which makes it difficult for journalists.

Still, I think the better newspapers in Singapore plod on in their efforts to bring good journalism to their readers. They tread a fine line in covering local politics and producing news reports and analyses as well as commentaries. These editors strive to keep their newspapers credible. That means honest writing and a balanced approach to issues, putting across different views and perspectives. In doing this, there is sometimes a need to push back the OB markers and create more space for discussion.

Such an approach means treading on the sensitive toes of the government more often. It keeps readers more tuned in and the papers usually growing in reach and credibility.

But it can also mean the careers of such editors do not run the full length. Changes can be made, and they are made, in a subtle and indirect manner. Cause and effect cannot be linked so easily.

Singapore is now at a crossroads in terms of journalism, newspapers and their credibility and survival. The mainstream media, led by the *Straits Times*, is steadily losing ground in readership and credibility. This is partly of their own making, as the newspapers here tend to take the path most trodden, keeping the powers-that-be relatively happy.

Meanwhile, social media is growing and Google and Facebook have become not just news aggregators; they have also become the places where numerous discussions take place in a relatively free and unrestrained manner. People are spending more time online and being influenced by what they see, hear and read. Some hardly spend time watching free-to-air TV or reading the newspapers.

Social media can be inaccurate and misleading, but then the MSM or mainstream media is losing credibility too, as it is seen as too one-sided and reflecting mainly the official or government view. The pervasiveness of social media has forced the government to adopt a higher profile in recent years and it is now not uncommon for ministers and government bodies to have their own Facebook profiles and pages.

The big question is whether nation-building journalism, conceived in the 1960s, will continue to hold sway. The context is radically different today. First we had the revolution of the internet; next, the sub-revolution of social and other online media. We are also witnessing the tech or digital revolution expanding into areas from manufacturing to retail to healthcare. As one online commentary by "Subrathiru" expressed so cogently: "The future economy is not going to tie in well with a model of authoritarian control. Free-spiritedness and creative thinking will be the currency of the future. There is obviously a realisation within policy circles that we need to get prepared for technological disruption. The only problem is that while everyone foresees disruption, nobody is willing to take bold steps to free up this society."

To build a vibrant landscape of innovation that the government constantly puts forth as its goal, we need to build a vibrant landscape of the mind. This can only happen with a free press, which is so central to the ideas and discourse within a society. Stifle the press and you stifle discussion on so many burning issues – and then you stifle the human mind, human inventiveness. It is simply impossible to have an intellectually open society without a free press, or to have an innovative society that is not intellectually open. Not even the most capable ministers in the world can square this circle.

Anyway, it appears that technology has rendered this whole discussion moot. The internet is a beast that cannot be tamed, unless Singapore wants to put up a Great Firewall like China, destroying its aspirations to be a hub for data and

WALKING TALL

An ode to a short editor who made it big at TODAY

Neil Humphreys

A CHANGE looked on the cards for some time.

Industry observers said there was a need for new leadership and greater synergy across all platforms to generate better media coverage.

When you're in the public eye, you are constantly aware of the brand's image and the need to strengthen it if you are to become the region's top player.

But enough about the perils of my favourite team, West Ham United — let's talk about my favourite Singapore newspaper instead.

Like the Hammers (my Premiership team, not the political party), the winds of change have been blowing through the TODAY newsroom and Caldecott. In the last fortnight, MediaCorp has made more changes than Liverpool manager Rafa Benitez.

But I'm not here to talk about all the personnel changes. Partly because it'll mean very little to the average reader; and partly because I'd get the sack. (Editor's disclaimer: We don't know where Neil got that idea from. Honestly.)

TODAY's editor-in-chief Mano Sabnani has decided to take a break from the shenanigans of the newsroom, so I thought I'd recognise his contribution to Singapore's media landscape.

Now, the first thing I must point out about Mano is he's not the tallest guy on the block.

When we were first introduced, I thought he was standing in a hole. Whenever we posed together in company photos, you either got the top of his head, or my navel.

But for a diminutive guy, he had big ambitions. Shortly after he took over as editor, he asked to see me. I was apprehensive. My column had been running for over a year by then and I thought he might pull the plug.

I can't recall my subject matter for the previous week's effort, but it was probably something innocuous like the *gahmen*, Romancing Singapore, homophobia, maid abuse, censorship or, the most controversial of them all, my mother.

"Neil, have you got a minute," he asked.

Of course, I replied, and removed my shoes.

Colleagues often wondered why I walked around the TODAY newsroom in my socks. Well, I can finally reveal the truth. It was to make Mano feel taller.

"It's about your column," Mano said, rather tentatively. Here it comes, I thought.

"My children really like it, so can I get a signed copy of your books for them?"

My relief was palpable. Although he never did pay me for those books.

And for a man who has spent a lifetime involved in investment banking and business journalism, Mano never offered me a single tip on the stock market.

Indeed the only financial tip I can recall was his suggestion to take France in this year's World Cup Final. Mano knows football like I know investment banking.

But he knows a fair bit about newspapers and he's a major reason why you're still able to read this one.

TODAY had already made great strides when Mano took over in 2003, but journalists from rival media organisations still referred to it as the "loss-making TODAY".

Stories appeared with introductions like: "MediaCorp's in-the-red newspaper TODAY, which is still in the red, announced at a press conference this morning that it is still in the red."

A little later, those same journalists were forced to drop the adjectival "loss-making" because TODAY broke even in 2005, so they started describing the daily as the "freesheet TODAY", which was rather unkind because it sounded like a brand of toilet paper.

Earlier this year, the paper recorded a profit in excess of $5 million and just last week, an independent survey revealed that TODAY is the second most-read newspaper in Singapore, with 571,000 readers.

It's becoming increasingly difficult for rival publications to prefix TODAY with an unflattering adjective. And it's rumoured that if those writers prefix TODAY with anything positive, they'll be taken round the back and shot.

Mano is a major reason for their dilemma.

TODAY's Napoleon (not because Mano is French, but because Napoleon was a short leader) guided the newsroom into the history books.

It's worth repeating that TODAY is the only newspaper not controlled by the Singapore Press Holdings to survive and thrive. What you're reading right now represents an alternative of sorts and Singaporean consumers must cherish alternatives.

Mano encouraged a wider spectrum of "voices" in the paper: Authoritative, social and humorous.

Most importantly, TODAY is the only paper in Singapore that doesn't take itself so damn seriously.

So raise your newspapers in a toast to a man who played a significant role in helping TODAY make media history.

Mano Sabnani.

Very talented.

Very short.

At the end of my stint at *TODAY* in 2006, Neil Humphreys wrote a cheeky piece on me – "a short editor who made it big".
Image reproduced with permission of © MediaCorp Press.

Celebrating *TODAY*'s fifth anniversary with the paper's key staff.

turning away many of the foreign talents it needs to remain at the cutting edge of knowledge. In recent times, websites offering highly independent, critical and persuasive commentary have proliferated online. Paradoxically, the more the government restrains the mainstream media, the more it will lose its credibility and effectiveness as a vehicle for the government to persuade the people and build the nation.

With all due respect, the government needs to radically change its policy on the media before change is forced upon it. This adaptation to the times will necessarily entail a degree of disorder, even chaos, that the Singapore government is known to abhor. But as Charles Darwin once wrote, "It is not the strongest of the species that survives, nor the most intelligent. It is the one most adaptable to change."

*   *   *

It was a hard slog at *TODAY*, wearing both the CEO and Editor-in-Chief hats. But there was satisfaction when I got home with the empty tiffin, which my dear wife prepared for me each day so that I would not miss my dinner, knowing that I had done my work. I was tired but I was happy, and I could sleep well.

It was unfortunate that my tenure at *TODAY* ended the way it did. But I can look back with pride at my almost four years helming the paper. When I went full-time into *TODAY* in April 2003, it was bleeding badly, but by 2006, the paper was well into the black, was well-read, and had garnered the attention of many quarters. It was perhaps unfortunate that *TODAY* was put in the spotlight, but if I were to view it positively, it meant that we had made good strides.

Chapter 7

FAMILY VALUES AND ROLES

THE BULWARK OF my endeavour at *TODAY* was none other than Nisha, my wife of 25 years by 2006. Like my mother in the first 13 years of my life, she gave unstinting support through thick and thin.

The two women in my life have both been full-time homemakers for the best part of their lives. My mother was always there for us when we were growing up. Although she had her own social life, most of her day was devoted to the home, her husband and the children. My wife Nisha is the same. She used to work as a kindergarten teacher in Jakarta before we got married in April 1981. Thereafter, she has been a full-time homemaker, taking care of the household, and subsequently, our children's needs.

I met Nisha through her maternal auntie, who was known to our family. One day, in February 1980, she turned up at our house, giving the excuse that she had visited the wrong house. We never turned guests away, so my father invited her in. I was at home that morning, getting ready for work. The auntie started small talk and was soon asking me about myself and my work. I had my breakfast and excused myself.

Our community is a small one, and everyone knows nearly everyone. It was common knowledge that I was working in the media and was still single then. At that time, I was almost 30 years old, and busy with my work in *BT*. Dada was putting pressure on me to get married and have a family; my two older brothers were already fathers and even my father had had two more children with my stepmother. The elders had introduced a few other girls to me but none of them worked out. I preferred to just concentrate on my work.

I had a few girlfriends in university and at work, but there was nothing too serious. The only relationship in earnest was with a girl I had met in university. We went out for a while and she joined me for part of my overland trek from Singapore to London in 1977. En route, she became good friends with an Irish guy we met, and eventually they became quite close. She and I went our separate ways in Europe. I was quite upset at how things had not worked out. We were of the same age; she wanted to get married but I was still footloose, wanting to travel and not ready to settle down. At that time, we were 27 years old and had known each other for about five years. The "break-up" was a blow. I felt a bit let down and realised how heart-wrenching relationships can be. My friend M Narayanan, a student in London, told me to get over it; life goes on, he said. So I steeled myself. When I came back to Singapore, I focused on work, I was not keen to get involved in anything else. I was quite happy for it to be that way.

As it turned out, the auntie was keen to introduce her 26-year-old niece, Nisha, to me. Nisha came from a middle-class Sindhi family in Indonesia. Her parents had initially made a home in Solo in Java, but later moved to Jakarta, which was a bigger city and a better place for business. Her father, Ramchand Nathani, a textile merchant, had eight children (five girls and three boys) to look after with his wife Shanta. Nisha – or Maya, as she was known then (it is a tradition among Hindu Sindhi females to adopt a new name after marriage, as mentioned in Chapter 1) – was the eldest.

I met Nisha when she came to Singapore, and we went out a few times. I liked her and we enjoyed our outings. So we got betrothed in April 1980. Both families wanted us to get married soon, in keeping with the Hindu tradition, but I told them that marriage would have to wait. I had a posting in London waiting for me, and I wanted to travel a little more. My London posting was with the *Investor's Chronicle*, which was part of the Economist group of publications, for five to six months. After that, I went to the United States and did a four-week cross-country tour from New York to Los Angeles via the South. I only returned to Singapore near the end of 1980.

Nisha and I got married on 24 April 1981. Our wedding was a simple one. The ceremony was held at a Sikh temple (Hindu Sindhis have historically had a close relationship with Guru Nanak, the founder of Sikhism) in Wilkinson Road, and we hosted a reception at the Sindhu House in Mountbatten Road a few days later. Our wedding was quite different

Nisha and I at our engagement ceremony at the Katong
Gurdwara (Sikh temple), April 1980.

At our wedding reception at Sindhu House, April 1981.

from some of the more traditional Sindhi weddings; we didn't have the Sangeet – the song and dance event before the wedding proper. Our families were not that well off, and I made it clear I did not want anything from Nisha's family. Our honeymoon was to Lake Toba (in Sumatra, Indonesia) for five days. A couple of years later, when I had more savings, we took a longer, second honeymoon to Europe where we toured 13 countries over eight weeks.

Being matchmade worked out for Nisha and me. Matchmade marriages in those days were not that different from a couple being introduced at a party or via Facebook in today's context. The couple has time to meet and get to know each other before deciding whether to take the relationship to marriage level. Nisha and I spent our first few years of marriage getting to know each other, travelling when we could, and learning to live as a couple. We did not want to have any children in those early years. Nisha took up a secretarial course to keep busy during the weekdays as I worked long hours in the newsroom. We became more active in the local Sindhi community and Nisha adapted well, with new friends. She also felt at home, as we were still living with my father, his second wife and four younger brothers (including two half-brothers from my stepmother).

Nisha provided me with stability and a partner with whom I could share experiences. For instance, she came with me to the UK when I did my Press Fellowship in Wolfson College, Cambridge, from January to March 1986. We shared a house with a few other international journalists. During the week, I'd work on my paper, which was on the topic of electronic newspapers. At that time, these were already emerging in the US. Digital was the way to go for the US because the suburbs and houses were quite spread out. The newspapers were experimenting with electronic versions to offset the costs of delivery. In those days, the internet was not so pervasive and developed, and electronic papers were more in the format of an email or HTML. It was like a very long email. Photos were still relatively rare in electronic formats and PDF was uncommon. I argued that the electronic newspaper would catch on because of improving technology. But at that time it was quite tiring for readers to go through an e-paper. And while e-papers were efficient in terms of distribution and printing costs, there were consequences on advertising from having no print copies. While in Cambridge, I also participated actively in campus life, attending numerous seminars and conferences, as well as the regular dinners in the college hall to meet with other academic staff and researchers.

While I was working on my paper and research, Nisha got involved with exercise and hobby courses in the Cambridge community centres. During the weekends, we would drive in our second-hand car around the Cambridge area to explore. Often, we would also drive down to London to visit my sister and her family.

After the completion of the fellowship, I did a secondary project on the biotechnology industry in Northeast England. It was traditionally the rust belt with its coal and shipbuilding industries. At that time, the area was transitioning into the new biotech industry and I was interested to see what it was all about.

After that, we decided to take a driving trip to Scotland. That year, the winter was severe. March was especially bad, with heavy sleet and wind. We had reached Edinburgh and were contemplating whether to push on further north. But we did not have the necessary cold-weather equipment for ourselves or for the car. Without snow tyres, we felt it was safer not to risk it and headed to the Lake District instead. The day after we reached the Lake District, there was a power failure due to extreme weather. We decided not to push on with the trip and to return to London. The B&B owner gave us directions to the highway, but we took a shortcut through the mountains (the Pennine Chain) in the hope that we could get there faster. The road was narrow and the blizzard was coming on. We were stuck on the road and decided to wait. The snow was piling up, it was getting colder and there was no one around. Nisha and I were thinking that was the end of us. We were getting really worried. As it always happens, when things seem to be at their bleakest, a ray of light appears. A truck came along and gave us directions to another highway. It was not the one we wanted to be on, but it was a start. We made it, and after some detours, managed to get back safely to Cambridge, quite thankful that we were alive.

Our children are god-sent

Our three children were god-sent. When we decided to try for children, we were not successful for a few years. We went to see various doctors and sought treatment but nothing worked. We tried the IVF route, but after a few unsuccessful attempts, we gave up. By our fifth or sixth year of marriage, we had stopped trying for children. Que sera sera, we told ourselves.

One day in office, I received a call from my friend Gowrie Manoghari, who called to pitch a story about a Dr V Atputharajah (Dr Rajah), a gynaecologist at KK Hospital who had written a book on sexual problems among Asian couples. In the end we featured him in the lifestyle section of *BT*. Gowrie later called to thank me when the story was picked up by various media. It was during that phone call that she asked about our situation, and suggested that we consult Dr Rajah.

We did. Dr Rajah went through our files and gave me a call one day to ask me to go down to see him at the hospital. I thought it was a serious matter. It turned out that Nisha's womb was tilted, which made it difficult for her to get pregnant in the conventional way. He suggested a workaround,

Proud parents of first-born Natasha in 1988.

Natasha with then Deputy PM Goh Chok Tong.

which did not involve any medical procedure, which we adopted.

In 1988, our first child, Natasha, was born. Our two sons, Karan and Dev, followed shortly afterwards, in 1989 and 1992. Dr Rajah delivered all our children, and we made him the godfather of the kids. Gowrie – without whom our children would not be here – is their godmother.

Is the modern woman happy?

Nisha has always been there for me and for our children. Her love for children and cooking has been consistent all these years. She has been instrumental in maintaining harmony and warmth in the home, even as I focused on the heavy routine of a newspaper editor for the large part of my working life. I could concentrate on my work because there was an assurance that she would mind the home and children to the best of her ability. In fact, she took it beyond that to ensure that I had home-cooked food to eat while working late in the office Mondays to Fridays.

Our division of duties has worked well, even though casual observers often question my reduced role in household duties. My focus on career ensured that there was sufficient bread for the family and some reserved for the future. I cleared my personal chores and mail on Saturdays by 5 p.m. and ensured Saturday evenings and the best part of Sundays were available for Nisha and the children in whatever activity.

(I would return to editing on Sunday evenings, to clear the paper for Mondays.)

Having a full-time mother at home makes all the difference. Nisha is always there for the children, and there are things that sometimes a domestic helper or nanny cannot resolve. I did wonder whether Nisha should have taken up full-time work in some organisation and built her own career. Did she have any choices? More importantly, would she have been happier with her life if she had to balance career/work with minding a household and children?

These are important questions which affect every family. Should families strive for a dual income, with both partners working full-time and at the same time sharing the home and family load equally? For some decades now, and especially since the end of World War II, there has been a global trend to push for equal rights for women across the globe. Equal rights means many things to different people, but a key thrust by many governments as well as NGOs has been the education of women.

Girls are still denied a full education in many countries, but in modern secular states like Singapore, they have had equal opportunity on this front even before our independence in 1965. Financial help in the education sector is available to both boys and girls right up to university. A happy consequence has been that women have been able to realise their full potential in various fields, including major professions like medicine, accountancy, architecture, law and engineering. Many are in business management and special-ised sectors like psychology, veterinary science and teaching.

Many countries, like Singapore, have encouraged young women to enter the workforce upon the completion of their education. Conventional thinking is that women should make use of the education they have gained to embark on full-time careers and contribute to the overall economy as well to the family. Where economies are doing well and the labour market is tight, having more women join the work-force has helped to meet the demand from businesses and professions as well as the public sector.

It has become the norm in modern societies like Singapore that a high proportion of women work and contribute to the economy. Families consequently enjoy a dual income with husband and wife both contributing to the coffers. The workload at home, such as cleaning and cooking as well as the minding of kids, if any, has to be shared. Dual-income families would, on average, also enjoy a higher aggregate income than single-income families, where one spouse, usually the husband, works full-time while the other spouse, usually the wife, is full-time at home taking care of all related matters, including children. In Singapore, and many other countries, the governments involved have bent backwards to assist and incentivise women to enter and then stay in the workforce, even after they become mothers. Extended maternity and sick leave as well as income tax rebates and outright cash grants have been given to women in the workforce. They pay subsidised rates for domestic helpers or enjoy lower government levies. The maids are expected to mind the children while the parents are at work.

In theory, the modern woman should be able to balance work life with her duties at home. She has domestic help and her husband is expected to share in the household chores and childcare duties. She should be happy with her own income and financial independence as well as recognition in the workplace and society. But is that really the case? I am no expert in this field and cannot produce original research which challenges the conventional wisdom about the role and priorities of modern women. I am sure many women heavily involved in their careers will say they are happy – and happier than they would be if they were stay-at-home moms.

But I think there is a proportion who find it difficult and stressful trying to balance a full-time job with the demands of a household. In many cases, I suspect, the men are not able or willing to play their role in sharing household and child-minding duties. It would be easy to say the problem lies with the underperforming men in such cases and to blame them for the stressed condition of the women involved. However, I think there is merit in considering how families have functioned through the ages, before the seismic changes that we now see became prevalent. Men were, traditionally, the hunter-gatherers or breadwinners of the family. Women would mind the home and family. If there was a farm to be tended to, the men would take the lead while the women would be the helpers, with their priority the home and family. Amidst all the talk of equality, we should remember that men and women traditionally form a good partnership because they complement each other, and you can only complement each other if you are different. If man is hunter and woman is nurturer, that works. If the woman becomes a hunter, the man will have to be the nurturer. A partnership of two hunters or two nurturers is not likely to be successful.

The negative side of a clear division of duties between male and female spouses was that the men were the sole breadwinners and the women depended on them for a livelihood. This, at times, led to the men overly dominating the family and leaving few decisions to the women. Worse, women had few options when the men decided to ill-treat them or leave them. A lack of education and financial means led to some women leading unhappy lives while remaining married.

I believe there are merits in adopting the traditional role division. I have been privileged that my mother and my wife both became full-time homemakers after they got married, and my family and I have benefited from that. I believe their lives have been fairly fulfilling. I think the traditional division of duties between spouses can work well even in the modern era of rising costs of living and the educational demands on children. In fact it could work even better than the shared-roles approach many couples adopt, where both work and share household chores. The sacrifice really is in

My 43rd birthday, 1993. Kids attacking the cake!

Nisha has always loved to dance – here she is (above left) performing at a Deepavali event at Sindhu House, 1999, and (above right) at the wedding of her youngest sister, Soni.

household income. But the reward is that duties are clear and once the work is done, the family can enjoy time together. If happiness in the family is the goal, then this is a serious option to consider.

Children at the heart of family

When the children arrived, we involved them in everything. In 1990, I was again due for an overseas course, this time to do the Advanced Management Programme at INSEAD Business School in France. By then, Natasha and Karan were born, and they came to France together with Nisha and me. We took the opportunity to explore Fontainebleau, with the Palace of Napoleon, and its surrounds, including Paris. Once, on a visit to Paris, by the time we were ready to get home, it was late. We tried catching the last train back, but the confusion over language and platform caused us to miss it. In those days, the stations were not as well kept or brightly lit as they are today. We had two kids with us, some bags and a camera. We chose to take a taxi back. It was costly, but it got us back to the campus at Fontainebleau safely and rather speedily.

For me, it was important to involve the children in our family life, to give them a sense of belonging and a sense of ownership. For instance, when we were looking to buy a house in the late 1990s, the whole family was involved in the decision-making process. The children would come with Nisha and me to see houses every weekend. Karan would make notes of every house we visited, including details like address, floor space and layout. After each visit, we'd evaluate the house together and discuss what we liked or didn't like.

Incidentally, though, when I bought our present house, our children were not involved. The opportunity came serendipitously. We had been looking around for a while, and a couple of potential transactions fell through. One day, a friend, Naffi, who was in the real estate business, alerted me to a potential fire sale. I saw the house together with Nisha, at short notice, and made the decision to buy it. It was a good price. Our children were none too happy about being caught unawares, but once they saw the house, they knew it would be their home for a long time. Thankfully, the deal went through and we have lived here ever since.

Another critical decision in which the children played a part was when I was debating whether to leave the position of Chief Editor and CEO of *TODAY* in late 2006. Natasha was then 18, Karan 17 and Dev just 14. We discussed the pros and cons. Their advice was that I needed to be happy and the income from the job was secondary as we had built up some reserves for the family. Nisha was also in agreement with them and I left MediaCorp without another job in hand.

*   *   *

All dressed up for Janmashtami (Lord Krishna's birthday), September 1996: (from left) my late cousin-sister Roop Mahtani, Karan, Natasha, Nisha, and Dev.

My 50th birthday, 2000. The children (left to right): Karan, Dev and Natasha.

One of the traits I've always tried to inculcate in my children is independence – in thought, action and financial standing. They do not have to be mavericks, but I always tell them it's a good thing to have a mind of their own. I'm quite an independent person, and mostly depend on myself. I do not expect my children to support me in any way when I get older. I make sure I have my own way of looking after myself and my wife. I always tell my children that it's a disadvantage to be brought up in a privileged family. They are not hungry enough to fight for things, and they may often take the easy way out. Many such children are not independent, not challenged enough as they intuitively know they can always fall back on the family for support and finances. Even simple things like going to school – many kids these days take taxis or Uber to get from place to place. Or they depend on their mothers to fetch them in the family car to and fro.

Nisha and I did not come from well-to-do families. We learned to make do with what we had. We have been lucky to get to where we are today, through hard work. We are still prudent with our expenditure. On the other hand, we try to be generous to the needy and give to charity. Money is something we can work for honestly, and one should always save some for a rainy day. That is a legacy of my Boy Scouts days, to always be prepared.

We always tell the children that there are a few things they should keep in mind: to have a belief in God, have integrity in everything they do, and have respect for family traditions and elders. It's important that Nisha and I lead by example, not just through talk.

Sibling unity is the key to family harmony

Another anchor which we remind ourselves to work for is the unity of the family. A stable family is necessary for a fulfilling life. Filial piety is important, and so is sibling unity. I'm not morally perfect but I try my best to lead by example. When my father was alive – and when Nisha and I started living on our own – I made it a point to visit him and my stepmother regularly. We'd bring a little something as a gesture and we made sure the children spent quality time with their grandparents. Nisha and I go to the temple regularly, and we bring the children along, as our parents did. Now that they have grown up, there are times when they'd rather do their own thing. But the one time they will all turn up is at the annual prayer that Nisha and I sponsor at the temple in memory of our deceased parents.

Today they still come to our room and chat with us at the end of the day. That, I'd like to think, is a testimony to our stable family ties. It is said that the family that eats together and prays together, stays together. We try to have meals together as often as possible, despite everyone's busy days.

I think there is a clear advantage in having a girl as a first-born. Natasha as the eldest child plays her role well. She has led the way forward for the boys in education and other aspects, with her gentle and persuasive manner. She tries to maintain good relationships with other family members and relatives. Boys are boys, and can be more independent-minded and assertive. Under the family's umbrella, Karan has grown to be an independent young man who is wise with money and the ways of the street. Dev is a mix of the two, gentle at times and very strong-willed on occasion.

Their personalities may be different, but my sense is that they look out for each other. When one sibling is in a difficult situation, or a decision needs to be made on some important matter, they will all offer their best thoughts, if consulted. For Nisha and me, our deepest hope is that the children will continue to support each other through life, even when we are no longer around to offer advice or participate.

Chapter 8

LIFE DOESN'T JUST HAPPEN, DOES IT?

FAITH IS AN important part of my life. I am not overly religious but I have deep respect for my parents' beliefs. I believe that in bringing up children, we need to anchor them in something. Faith is one such anchor. Life doesn't just happen. A friend, Wan Hsin-hun, once said something that I found so pithy yet powerfully persuasive: "I don't believe that everything we have is caused by the random collision of atoms." The purposefulness of living organisms, the human brain, even a single cell, are so phenomenal that it is hard to believe that it all formed randomly. There is also not a shred of empirical evidence that purposeful machines and structures can develop through random events – it would be akin to pieces of metal, plastic and glass randomly coming together to become a smartphone. That is something we have to acknowledge and have respect for.

When we discuss God, we need to first acknowledge the possibility of such a reality. Further, is it possible there are many gods in different forms or manifestations? Different religions profess different prophets or representatives of

God, and some religious philosophers consider themselves an incarnation of God. Who is right or holds the truth?

I don't profess to know all the answers to these difficult questions, as we do not have all the answers to questions about life on Earth and the complexities of the universe beyond Earth. How did it all come about and is there someone or something who made it all happen and facilitated the pattern of life we see on Mother Earth, or Gaia as it is known in Greek mythology? For me, the human mind has not reached a stage where we understand all about the universe and the creation of planets and how some of these planets attain the right combination of elements and atmosphere to sustain life.

Imagine you are one of the ants living in an anthill in a forest. To you, the anthill represents your entire world. You may not comprehend the other anthills in the vicinity or deeper recesses of the forest. You probably also cannot fathom the idea that there are different species of ants, or that their size, eating and living habits and lifespan are quite different from yours. If an animal or human trampled on your anthill, by accident or deliberately, it would seem like the end of the world for you. The loss of life would be tremendous and even if you survived the destruction of your anthill, your life would be irrevocably changed as you rebuilt your home with the other survivors of the anthill disaster. Philosophically, you might think it was an act of God; an ant-God that was punishing your colony for some misdeed, perhaps. It would be hard for you to imagine that there are many thousands of anthills like yours in that forest, and many other living creatures more powerful than you who could determine your future. Multiply that by the number of forests on Earth and you see it is impossible for ants to get the big picture.

For us humans, we take much pride in our intelligence and ability to reason. So I don't expect everyone to agree with my simple reasoning presented here, which is based on a life of observing religions and their practices and the behaviour of practitioners. People are brought up from birth to adopt certain religions and philosophies. They naturally become resistant to alternatives which do not fit in with their narrative.

My arguments for the existence of God do not vary greatly from the famous Argument from Design and the Argument from First Cause. These arguments essentially establish a *possibility* that the universe came into being by design; in the absence of conclusive proof that this is untrue, we should keep an open mind to the possibility of a God.

Also relevant is an essay by my good friend Steven Ooi arguing that science does not provide a better answer than religion on the issue of the origins of the universe and of life. You can read it online at https://gptuitionsg.wordpress.com/2017/01/24/human-actions-should-be-based-on-scientific-fact-not-religious-faith-a-model-essay/

The history of religious practices shows that old beliefs are periodically replaced by new philosophies and practices.

We have seen how so-called pagan rituals and beliefs are replaced over time by so-called modern religions. The adherents of modern religions argue against superstition and usually claim to be more practical and logical. Yet, they too rely on what was said or written a long time ago and which is hard to verify or prove today.

But religion is mostly about faith, which is the evidence of things not seen, the substance of things hoped for, as the Bible puts it. Perhaps it is an intuitive bridge of belief that fills a void left by reason. And reason alone cannot answer many of our deepest questions of life. So the major faiths or religions continue to be highly influential and followed by billions around the world, even if sceptism resulting from scientific rationalism has turned a significant number away. The decline of communism has been a major positive for religions, with countries like Russia and China seeing a gradual revival of religious practices. These were previously strictly taboo in communist societies. So, there is growth in the major religions in some parts of the world and religiosity is also on the rise. People in many countries are becoming more religious as they adapt to the pressures of living in modern societies where morality and ethical values are seen as being threatened by the pervasiveness of capitalism and the rat race. The positive side of such trends is that people have something to fall back on in stressful periods of their lives. They may not practise all that their religions teach all the time, but the back-up is always there at the back of their minds. Religions mostly urge people to live good lives – caring for their families; giving to the poor; staying honest and hardworking; looking after mind and body; and respecting parents and ancestors.

Some of the writings in the old books may need updating; there are unsavoury aspects in most holy books. Those bits were put on the record because thousands of years ago, they were deemed necessary. If a strident approach was taken to non-believers in the books, it may have been necessary at that time as a defensive measure. Today, thousands of years later, that attitude may be outdated. Most of us would agree that context is important to proper understanding of anything we read – we should not forget to apply this principle when reading our religious texts as well.

These unsavoury aspects of the holy books may give rise to tensions between different religious groups. Some faiths claim their way is the only way to God and all other ways lead to a miserable afterlife. Or rebirth. This attitude needs to be moderated by the leaders of the various faiths. But this is easier said than done. Men and women who profess to know God are often themselves caught in tunnel vision. Like the ants in the anthill, they are unable to comprehend alternative concepts of God and related beliefs. Their lives and careers are often embedded in their religions, and so selfish personal motives come into play.

A secular approach to religion

Yes, the tension among religions has to be moderated. The only way forward for nations is to adopt a secular approach to religions and treat them as personal preferences. Countries like Singapore and India have secular constitutions that put the rule of law at the top of society. Citizens and residents are allowed to practise what they like so long as their beliefs do not get in the way of other citizens and the rule of law.

This approach is workable in the long run. Different races and religions can co-exist within the boundaries of a single nation if mutual tolerance and understanding are practised. This, in turn, allows for different people to work together for the betterment of their nation and, with that, their own lives. But again, this is easier said than done. Career politicians often use religion and/or race to appeal to the primordial instincts of voters. When enough people listen to them, the result is divided societies and endless conflicts or even civil wars. No one gains in such prolonged conflicts for supremacy, as we see in the Middle East and the Israeli-Palestinian conflict today.

People have to understand that some religions and beliefs may also have limited lifespans. As scientists gain more knowledge of the Cosmos and the origins of the universe as well as life on other planets, old concepts and beliefs may have to be abandoned. As in the ant analogy, we do not yet fully comprehend many things about life and the universe. Why should it have to be that man is superior to all other living forms on Earth, for example? What gives us the right to kill and eat different animals without any sense of guilt?

The universe out there is so wide and large that we have yet to understand its extent. We know a little about our own galaxy but there are thousands, if not millions, of galaxies out there which we do not have an iota of information about. It is very likely and possible that there are many, many stars out there that have planets with life forms circulating around them. These life forms would thrive on the same elements found on Earth: water and oxygen in a conducive atmosphere.

I believe that life beyond Mother Earth or Gaia is a near-certainty. Further, it is very likely indeed that there are dozens, if not more, Earth-like planets that have intelligent life forms. Their development may even be far ahead of us humans and so it is not science fiction to imagine that these intelligent life forms may also be trying to check out the rest of the universe. It is just that they have not reached us and we, too, do not have the means to reach them. But it has to happen at some point. Or perhaps it has happened in the long past of human history, in past great civilisations, but we do not have clear records. Some clues are provided in great ancient monuments like Machu Picchu in Peru, the Pyramids in Egypt, and Stonehenge in the United Kingdom.

When the time comes that we are able to connect with distant civilisations in the universe, then the whole concept of God will change again. Humans need not be at the centre of the concept of God. He or She or It would be the creator of all the different life forms in the universe, with different levels of intelligence. God would be seen as the force that created the whole universe, with its millions of galaxies and stars with planetary systems that support and promote life.

Nature is God; omnipotent

The Earth, our beloved Gaia, would then be seen as a mere speck in the great scheme of things – a little anthill in a great forest on Earth with many forests and thousands if not millions of anthills. I, the little human with some intelligence, am just one of these ants living in a vulnerable anthill, with no clear understanding of the big picture. What we can do is to understand our own limitations. Accept that there is a possibility of God and that he is omnipotent and omnipresent. In other words, he created everything in the vast universe and is all-encompassing, and Mother Earth is just one planet that supports life. Our purpose in life is to live a good one and to minimise the damage to Mother Earth in the process.

We can take what we need to live and grow. But there is no need to accumulate great wealth at the expense of other living things or Mother Earth. That is not our role or right. Mother Earth is there for us and for future generations of humans and other life forms. Animals have just as much right to live and thrive on this Earth. Killing or hurting animals and destroying forests needlessly is akin to working against God's great plans. Most religions respect Nature and we should keep that in mind. God is the creator of the whole universe and is manifested in Nature. We are a part of Nature and there is a delicate balance on Earth between its inhabitants and the elements. Man is now reshaping the Earth with his technology and neverending needs; even greed. In the process, he is altering the delicate balance of elements on Earth. Nature is being forced back by Man and restricted to nature reserves and parks. But that is not the way it was intended, and Nature will fight back with a vengeance.

We need to be acutely aware that any creator is on the side of Nature. One could argue that God and Nature are one and the same. Destroy Nature and you are working against the omnipresent and omnipotent God – this is a concept not enough people understand. I can only hope this understanding of our minuteness, and the immensity and power of God and the universe, catches on among more thinking people. Before it is all too late and our anthill, Mother Earth, is vanquished.

Chapter 9

REFLECTIONS ON LIFE
IN SINGAPORE

I LOVE TREES. I grow them where I can – at home and in the neighbourhood. Not everyone appreciates my work. Still, I labour on. I grow them from seeds, cuttings and saplings. Shortly after I moved into where I live now, I planted a local Sakura or Trumpet tree from seed. I did not imagine how big it would grow! It had an advantageous position in the garden, where it got good sunlight and more than its fair share of water. It stood like a giant near the stand pipe and our main gate. During its season in May, and often at other times too, it would shower the porch with pink flowers. Those flowers and seeds would then germinate into young trees.

In April 2016, I had to trim it down. It had outgrown the garden. All the branches were cut off, leaving only the main trunk. True to character, it did not give up and within six months, it was growing a profusion of branches and leaves again.

To provide for diversity in our small garden, it had to be removed totally. So the death knell came in April 2017. I hired two groups of people to remove the tree. The first group failed; could only do the young branches. A second group came and cleaned out the trunk with chainsaws.

So our great Sakura tree is no more. Its shade is gone, after 15 years of life. The younger plants and trees now have a better chance to share the sun and water. It will be a rejuvenated, more diverse garden, I hope.

I'd like to think the tree did not live in vain. Over the last 15 years, it provided my family with much joy. Its flowers decorated our garden and its canopy was home to many birds, whose company my wife and I enjoyed when they came to roost.

In the past 20 years or so, our garden has gone from bare to almost a mini forest of sorts. There's a sampling of all sorts of plants, from the more common orchids to hibiscus and jasmine, palms of a few types, to a neem tree, longans and edible plants such as bittergourds. It took a lot of trial and error, and experimenting over many weekends for the garden to grow to such maturity. Even now, I'm constantly pottering about the garden, trying out different plants.

Gardening is a creative activity and I think that appeals to me. Creating things or life forms. I am not good at artwork or painting. But writing appeals to me as an art form – essays and poems as well as analysis and commentary. Building a portfolio of stocks and nurturing them to fruition is also being creative, with a strong element of analysis.

Growing plants is also analytical and creative. One needs to pay attention to detail, including choosing the right

Neem tree that I planted from seed 15 years ago.

When our great Sakura tree outgrew our garden, 70-year-old Mr Jamal did a marvellous job of climbing and cutting stage by stage.

potting mixture, picking healthy seeds and positioning the plants correctly for growth. Poor-quality soil, too much or too little sun or water can set back the growth of a plant. As in picking investments, one needs attention to detail and loads of patience. Growth can be slow at first and accelerate later, given the right conditions. Then, unexpectedly, the plant can be hit by pests and almost die off unless the gardener is alert and knows what to do to rescue it. It is highly rewarding when the flowers bloom and the trees bear fruit. It is like watching your investments in small companies grow into big, dividend-paying stocks. Hard work and analysis pays off!

I'd like to think that my little garden, with over a hundred different plants, contributes to the overall big picture of a pretty, green Singapore.

Singapore: The beautiful Isle of Lakes

Singapore has had many names in its history. In ancient times, from the 14th century, it was known as Temasek. It was then a small trading port serving the Malay archipelago. Fortunes waxed and waned, and later on, when the Srivijayan prince Parameswara explored the island, he decided to call it Singa Pura, meaning Lion City in Sanskrit, the ancient Indian language. When Sir Stamford Raffles landed in Singapore and decided to make it a trading base for the British, he kept the name Singapura and anglicised it to Singapore. That name has been retained through the colonial period and when we were a part of Malaysia (1963–65) and now, as an independent nation.

But all the while, as a developing nation, we have also been searching for a nickname or caption that would stick for Singapore – something that the world could easily identify with the island republic.

In the 70s, the tourism authorities were pushing for Singapore to be known as "Instant Asia". That caught on and it did help bring more visitors to Singapore. Instant Asia meant a place where one could taste the culture and food as well as music and the arts of China, India, as well as Malaysia and Indonesia. Eventually, however, other countries also jumped on this bandwagon. Malaysia, for example, could also claim to be a melting pot of Asian cultures, the same features that brought people to Singapore.

In the 90s, we were talking about Singapore as a Garden City. The greening of the island had taken place, with all the hard work to clean up the streets, pave back lanes, have better walkways for pedestrians and reserving areas for parks and recreation. Trees lined most roads and the continuous "Keep Singapore Clean" campaign produced noticeable results.

Singaporeans were already living in a clean, green city. But the push to improve living conditions and the environment did not stop at that. With the strengthening of the National Parks Board and the expansion of its role and scope, the idea of a "City in a Garden" was mooted for the new millennium.

This was a leap forward from the Garden City concept. Where previously the planners were happy with tree-lined streets and shrubs everywhere as well as parks all around the island, the thinking shifted to developing the whole island as a garden with all the green areas linked by park connectors. The built-up areas are thus seen as set within a giant garden that is the island of Singapore. That is certainly a great concept and making it a reality has meant much work and expenditure. The park connector network is still being developed as I write this piece in 2017; it will take another seven or eight years to complete it and allow people to criss-cross the island on a bicycle or on two feet without having to go onto the main roads and highways.

This development, together with the expansion of the mass rapid transit (MRT) rail network to all corners of Singapore, will allow Singaporeans to leave their cars behind and move around freely on the MRT and via pathways and connectors. The network is also friendly to the disabled and elderly – ramps and lifts are available where needed.

At the same time, we have also had to ensure our rivers are clean. There has been a massive effort since the 1960s to clean up the Singapore River, Kallang River and Geylang River, for example. Systematically and painstakingly, the waterways have been cleaned up and their banks greened. The transformation of the rivers and their surrounds has been nothing short of outstanding. Today, the Singapore River area is a popular residential and entertainment area, no less desirable than other prestigious districts popular with tourists and locals.

The old, fetid and filthy Kallang and Geylang Rivers are today as clean and green as any other part of Singapore. Both have excellent walkways and tracks for cyclists and many new bridges have been built to facilitate the crossing of these rivers and general accessibility of the residential and recreation areas. Locals love it and so do visitors. Clean, green and safe. Our parks and connectors are well lit, for the enjoyment of families any time of the day.

There are other important developments that have not been so well noticed. Singapore's need for its own water resources has necessitated a continuous and massive effort to build up our ability to conserve water and increase the quantity in reserve. So, drains and other waterways have been used to collect water and channel it into reservoirs, instead of into rivers that flow into the sea.

Over the years, we have converted many rivers into reservoirs. Examples would be the Kranji, Upper Seletar, Lower Seletar and Murai reservoirs and Jurong Lake. In recent years, we have added Marina Reservoir to the list. This massive reservoir includes the Singapore River as well as the Kallang and Geylang Rivers. It would have been unimaginable 50 years ago that the Geylang River could one day be part of a reservoir from which part of the water needs of Singaporeans would be met. But that is a fact today: both the Kallang and Geylang Rivers are part of our fresh water catchment.

The reservoirs of Singapore form part of the overall effort to meet our rising water needs. The other major sources (in the Four Taps strategy) are (1) water from Johor in Malaysia; (2) recycled or NEWater; and (3) desalination of seawater.

An important consequence of the conversion of our natural rivers to reservoirs is that the island's ecology is changing. In the area where I live, in the east of Singapore, there is a visible change in the flora and fauna. The fresh water in the Kallang and Geylang Rivers means different plants and trees can thrive on the banks fed by the fresh water in the ground or nearby. It also means a ready source of water for birds, which have been gradually increasing in variety and number. Previously seldom-seen kingfishers and egrets are now commonly spotted in these areas. Even the rare Asian otters are now seen in various places in Singapore, thanks to the ready supply of fish for them in the various river reservoirs. The offshore islands, like Pulau Ubin and Pulau Tekong, are also becoming havens for birds and wildlife, thanks to the ready supply of fresh water and a natural, green environment.

So, while the world worries about climate change, overcrowding and pollution, Singapore is actually moving to be cleaner, greener and more receptive to flora and fauna than it has ever been since colonial times. Our human population has been increasing steadily, so that it is now more than three times what it was in the 1950s, when we attained self-government. Land use is more intensive and people live in high-rise buildings and condominium complexes. There are housing estates everywhere, and industrial and commercial complexes dot the island. Yet, the flora and fauna seem to have adapted to the dense human population and are thriving in the areas reserved for them as well as the parks and reservoirs shared with people.

Singapore is evolving into a beautiful Isle of Lakes – a tropical garden city built between these green lakes that have been created from the old flowing rivers of salty or sea water. We could promote this concept of Singapore as a tropical Isle of Lakes. Just as Venice is a city on water and Amsterdam has its canals, Singapore has its lakes along the lines of Hanoi in Vietnam and Udaipur in India. Lake cities have a pull of their own, offering living and recreation by the water. Singapore has shown that dense living need not be entirely at the expense of the environment; the two can go together. The clean, green lake environment can be a durable advantage for Singapore as it pushes towards being a truly global city.

I walk quite a lot in the area where I live. Brisk walking is a good form of exercise and I find it easy to take off on this activity, as it can be done anytime and requires little in the way of equipment. You just need a good pair of shoes, and you're off. In contrast, playing tennis or golf means you need partners and also a booking for the venue. These may not always be easy to come by.

I have witnessed first-hand the improvements in the infrastructure of this city-state. Our public servants are constantly at work, rebuilding bridges, improving pavements, lining streets and park connectors with trees, and providing rain shelters. Where space allows, facilities such as exercise points are built. It is evident that the improvements have attracted more people to frequent the parks and river walkways, for exercise and relaxation. This is in contrast to, say, the time of my parents, when we had to make our way to specific parks (like Katong Park and Marine Parade) to enjoy greenery and open spaces. Nowadays, there is a park and jogging track around every corner; Singaporeans just have to avail themselves of these facilities. These changes are for the better.

Singapore has body; needs more soul

My friend Steven Ooi says the infrastructure is in place. Aesthetic living is here. "Yet, where has the soul gone? Why is it the people you walk past in that gorgeous park on a beautiful morning cannot even smile and say hello? The pervasive hand of the state is everywhere – planting and fertilising trees, repairing basketball courts, catching mosquito breeding, doing job-matching for the unemployed. But it has reached a point where the people have little need to organise as a community and solve problems together anymore. You are one of the lucky few to own land in Singapore and be able to plant your own trees, Mano. The vast majority of us have to content ourselves with little boxes in the sky. If we plant a papaya tree beside our block, the government puts up a notice beside the lift with a picture of the offending tree, and the warning: "UNAUTHORISED PLANTING. Please remove immediately." I saw this with my own eyes, at my block. Is it any wonder that the people have lost a sense of ownership of the country and connectedness to one another?"

I agree that we have to put more soul into Singapore. All of us living in this city-state need to make the effort to make this a more caring, participative and inclusive society.

A small but important part of my own legacy is the Soul of Singapore (SoS) group on Facebook. It fills a very important need – a safe place for discussion of issues affecting Singapore. The rest of the internet is largely a wilderness where that's concerned – most forums and message boards are flooded by abusive posts whenever emotive Singaporean issues are in play. The moderation on SoS is done intelligently, in a rule-based and highly reasoned way but with a light touch so that it does not stifle free and honest conversation. The civilised yet reasonably liberal environment it provides has attracted many intellectuals and facilitated a very high standard of public discourse rarely seen on other online spaces. I believe strongly that Singaporeans should engage on issues that affect their lives – today and tomorrow. I hope you, my reader, will join this 8000-strong community and offer your views and suggestions for a better Singapore.

Balancing "HFCR" (Health, Family+Friends, Career, and the Right life): (top) at the *Business Times*, where I got my start in journalism, and made lifelong friends, including (left to right) Kenneth James, Salil Tripathi, Chuang Peck Ming, Anna Teo and Margaret Thomas; and (above) with the family at Karan's graduation from my alma mater in 2015.

FINAL THOUGHTS AND A HOME-COOKED PHILOSOPHY

SINGAPORE HAS CHANGED beyond recognition in my lifetime. Likewise, change has been very much a large part of my life – constantly trying new things and experiences, going on new adventures. Sometimes, the changes were unpleasant, but, on hindsight, they were all necessary. All of them were adventures in one way or another, learning curves that helped me understand the world and myself better.

There are a few people I'm especially grateful to, in terms of my learning curves: Peter Lim, Tan Soo Nan and Ernest Wong. Career-wise, these three people helped me tremendously. Peter was my colleague in the newsroom. When I knew him, he was the Editor-in-Chief of the English and Malay newspapers of the Straits Times Press. In my years in *BT*, and later *ST*, he provided much helpful insight and support. Peter always had time for colleagues and a listening ear. He would hear you out and offer options, as a colleague. There was no bossing around for him. Soo Nan, senior banker, was the man who roped me into DBS, opening a new avenue for me at a time when I was looking for change. He read my columns in *BT* and felt I could take DBS Securities to a new level in projecting its research and commentary on the markets. Ernest, the CEO of MediaCorp, was the man who introduced me to *TODAY*, where I spent almost four years working with a fantastic team of people, and where I saw its fortunes turn for the better.

Final reflections? Well, my life is not over yet. It is possible I will change my views on various matters as I go forward into old age. The hope is that my mind remains intact and balanced and that some ravaging disease does not render me intellectually incapacitated. I guess that is one of the reasons why it has become necessary to write my memoirs. It is the life of an ordinary man – one who grew up in Singapore and has seen it transform in many ways. The story of a successful Singapore has been told many times, but the story of ordinary people is less well known. How have they managed over the years and what values do they hold dear? I am sure others have equally, if not more, compelling stories to tell their family, friends and the world at large. They should do it, to put on record events of this memorable period for Singapore, since the end of World War II.

My approach to life has been to live it fully and meaningfully. Make maximum use of time and prioritise what needs to be done each day. Think before you act or make any decision; consider all angles. Once a decision has been made, stick by it until compelling evidence suggests it has to be reviewed. Problems are there every day. They are there to be solved. If the problem is beyond you, then let it be. Some higher authority or power will have to resolve it. Lastly, remember to enjoy life. It is short and you should not deny yourself the things you enjoy. Exercise moderation and you will be alright. Balance is important in life.

My own home-cooked formula is to balance HFCR (Health, Family, Career and living the Right life) for a successful life.

The first is Health. You need to look after it or nothing else matters. You can only look after your family if you are healthy yourself, physically and mentally. Avoid excesses and bad habits. Eat lightly and healthily. Vegetables, fruits and seeds/legumes/nuts are really what we need for our bodies to function properly. The rest, especially the whole range of man-made processed foods and drinks, are not vital.

Next comes Family. With your own good health, you will be able to grow your family and nurture each member to his or her full potential. Big doses of care and concern are needed. Relationships have to be nurtured painstakingly, starting with the immediately family and then going on to the extended family and relatives. Give and take is essential. I am still on the learning curve in these aspects!

The F in HFCR also stands for Friends: build your network and keep it through life.

Career comes next. With a stable family, you can build a business or career. Take an honest approach and you will have peace of mind. Eventually, colleagues and employees will trust and respect you. Customers and suppliers will prefer to deal with you on a long-term basis. Remember, there will be problems but they are there to be solved; building businesses and careers are long-term endeavours. A secondary meaning of C is Charity. It is essential that as we grow in our careers, we help worthy causes, where possible.

Finally, you need to live the Right life. That means standing up for what you believe in, after you have evaluated the alternatives. Avoid what is clearly wrong and unprincipled. Mistakes are fine, but get back on track as soon as possible.

So there you have it. HFCR. The way to an enjoyable and successful life. Anyone can do it!